How to Use This Book

Look for these special features in this book:

SIDEBARS, **CHARTS**, **GRAPHS**, and original **MAPS** expand your understanding of what's being discussed—and also make useful sources for classroom reports.

FAQs answer common **F**requently **A**sked **Q**uestions about people, places, and things.

WOW FACTORS offer "Who knew?" facts to keep you thinking.

TRAVEL GUIDE gives you tips on exploring the state—either in person or right from your chair!

PROJECT ROOM provides fun ideas for school assignments and incredible research projects. Plus, there's a guide to primary sources—what they are and how to cite them.

Please note: All statistics are as up-to-date as possible at the time of publication.

Consultants: William Loren Katz; Vagel C. Keller Jr., Visiting Professor of History, Carnegie Mellon University; Gene Ulmer, Professor Emeritus, Temple University

Book production by The Design Lab

Library of Congress Cataloging-in-Publication Data
Somervill, Barbara A.
 Pennsylvania / by Barbara A. Somervill.
  p. cm.—(America the beautiful. Third series)
 Includes bibliographical references and index.
 ISBN-13: 978-0-531-18588-9
 ISBN-10: 0-531-18588-5
 1. Pennsylvania—Juvenile literature. I. Title. II. Series.
 F149.3.S663 2009
 974.8—dc22   2007031121

1 2 3 4 5 6 7 8 9 10 R 18 17 16 15 14 13 12 11 10 09

AMERICA ★ THE ★ BEAUTIFUL

Pennsylvania

BY BARBARA A. SOMERVILL

Third Series

WITHDRAWN

Children's Press®
An Imprint of Scholastic Inc.
New York ★ Toronto ★ London ★ Auckland ★ Sydney
Mexico City ★ New Delhi ★ Hong Kong
Danbury, Connecticut

CONTENTS

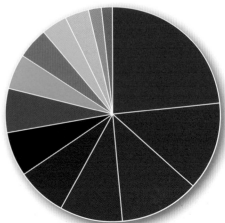

LAKE ONTARIO

CANADA

LAKE ERIE

NEW YORK

N W E S

0 ——— 40
Miles

ERIE

OHIO

Allegheny

The Andy Warhol
Museum

Carnegie Museum
of Natural History

Punxsutawney
Phil

Allegheny
Plateau

Penn State

Little League
Baseball Museum

Susquehanna

Lackawanna
Coal Mine

SCRANTON

WILKES-BARRE

Crayola Factory

W. Br. Susquehanna

WILLIAMSPORT

Susquehanna

PENNSYLVANIA

PITTSBURGH

Allegheny Mountains

Monongahela

HARRISBURG

Hershey's
Chocolate World

Gettysburg National
Military Park

ALLENTOWN

Valley Forge National
Historical Park

PHILADELPHIA

The U.S. Mint

Franklin
Institute
Science
Museum

NEW
JERSEY

Delaware

National
Watch & Clock
Museum

WEST
VIRGINIA

MARYLAND

Chesapeake Bay

Washington, D.C.

VIRGINIA

Delaware
Bay

DELAWARE

Independence
National
Historical Park

Welcome to Pennsylvania!

HOW DID PENNSYLVANIA GET ITS NAME?

PENNSYLVANIA

When William Penn arrived in Pennsylvania in 1682 to start a new colony, forests covered much of the land. Penn suggested the land be called Sylvania, from the English word *sylvan*, meaning "wooded." King Charles II of England wanted to honor Penn's father, Admiral William Penn, so he combined *Penn* with *Sylvania*. The combined word, Pennsylvania, means "Penn's woods." Although the younger Penn offered the king's secretary a bribe to change it, Pennsylvania is what the king wanted, and Pennsylvania is what it is called today.

8

READ ABOUT

Savantine Falls
in the Delaware
State Forest in
Pike County

CHAPTER ONE

LAND

★

IN PENNSYLVANIA, YOU'RE BOUND TO FIND SPECTACULAR SIGHTS AT EVERY TURN. Though it is small compared to most states, with an area of 46,055 square miles (119,282 square kilometers), Pennsylvania abounds with beauty. Its highest point, Mount Davis, rises 3,213 feet (979 meters) above sea level in Somerset County. The lowest point is at sea level along the Delaware River. From east to west, north to south, it is a land of stunning hills and valleys and breathtaking lakes, rivers, and waterfalls.

This fern fossil, found in a coal mine in St. Clair, dates to some 300 million years ago.

GEOLOGICAL HISTORY

Pennsylvania's geology has played a dramatic role in the state's history. Over millions of years, rich deposits of coal, iron, oil, and natural gas built up inside the earth.

From about 600 million to 240 million years ago, Pennsylvania lay under a shallow sea. Dense plant life filled swamps. As the plants died, they sank to the bottom, eventually forming thick layers. Over time, mud and sand covered the dead plants. Under pressure and heat over millions of years, the decayed plants became coal.

More than a century ago, **industrialists** began to take advantage of the area's natural resources to create enormous amounts of wealth for themselves and steady incomes for their workers. But they also created serious pollution, which Pennsylvanians struggle with to this day.

Pennsylvania Geo-Facts

Along with the state's geographical highlights, this chart ranks
Pennsylvania's land, water, and total area compared to all other states.

Total area; rank . . . . .46,055 square miles (119,282 sq km); 33rd
Land; rank . . . . 44,817 square miles (116,076 sq km); 32nd
Water; rank . . . . .1,239 square miles (3,209 sq km); 28th
Inland water; rank . . . . 490 square miles (1,269 sq km); 33rd
Great Lakes water; rank . . . 749 square miles (1,940 sq km); 7th
Geographic center . . . . 2.5 miles (4 km) southwest of Bellefonte
Latitude . . . . 39°43' N and 42° N
Longitude . . . . .74°43' W and 80°31' W
Highest point . . . . Mount Davis, 3,213 feet (979 m)
above sea level in Somerset County
Lowest point . . . . Sea level at the Delaware River
Largest city . . . . .Philadelphia
Longest river . . . . .Susquehanna

Source: U.S. Census Bureau

 **Rhode Island, the smallest state, could
fit inside Pennsylvania 30 times.**

LAND REGIONS

Pennsylvania is divided into six regions: the Atlantic
Coastal Plain, the Piedmont, the Ridge and Valley
Province, the New England Province, the Appalachian
Plateau, and the Central Lowlands.

Atlantic Coastal Plain

The Atlantic Coastal Plain is the smallest geographic
region in Pennsylvania. Philadelphia and the counties to either side of the city lie in this region. This
area rises from sea level to about 200 feet (61 m). The
region is carved by dozens of small creeks and streams
that feed the Delaware River. During the ice age, some

WORD TO KNOW

plateau *an elevated part of the
earth with steep slopes*

Pennsylvania Topography

Use the color-coded elevation chart to see on the map Pennsylvania's high points (dark red to orange) and low points (green to dark green). Elevation is measured as the distance above or below sea level.

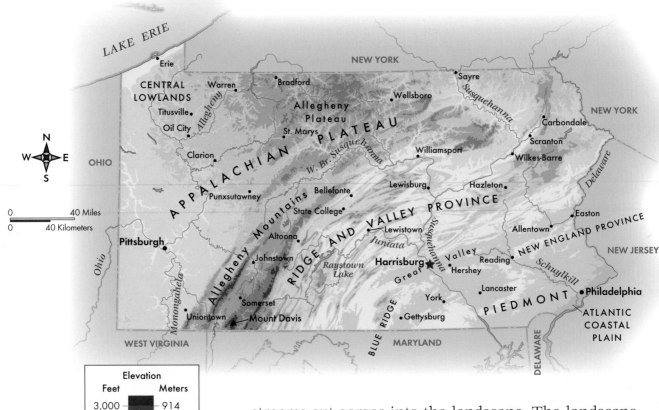

Elevation

Feet		Meters
3,000		914
2,200		671
1,400		427
600		183

streams cut gorges into the landscape. The landscape, once tidal marsh, is today gently rolling hills.

Piedmont

The Piedmont is rich farmland lying in a broad arc just above the Atlantic Coastal Plain. The land is 100 to 500 feet (30 to 152 m) above sea level. The Susquehanna River valley cuts through the western part of the Piedmont, and a small section of the Blue Ridge Mountains juts into the southwest corner.

The Susquehanna River, as seen from Hyner View State Park in Clinton County

Ridge and Valley Province

The Ridge and Valley landscape is a combination of sharp ridges, flat ridges, narrow valleys, and rich forestland. The region is also an arc, cutting from eastern Pennsylvania toward the southwest. Below the surface of the Ridge and Valley lie billions of tons of coal.

New England Province

In northeastern Pennsylvania, the Hudson Highlands of New York and the Ramapo Mountains of New Jersey connect to a small region of hills and ridges called the Reading Prong. Hills there are steep and rounded on the top.

The ground under Centralia, Pennsylvania, has been on fire since 1962. Fire in a garbage dump lit an underground coal vein, and the fire cannot be put out. The fire has turned Centralia into a ghost town.

SEE IT HERE!

WHITE-WATER RAFTING

Spring, summer, and fall, tourists flock to the Poconos and Lehigh Gorge for white-water rafting. The scenery is breathtaking, the rapids thrilling, and the trip a full five hours of energetic fun. Pennsylvania white-water rafting combines the best scenery with the thrills of a roller coaster ride. Put your bathing suit and life preserver on for this trip—you will get wet!

Appalachian Plateau

The Appalachian Plateau is Pennsylvania's largest region, covering most of the western and northern part of the state. It consists of several smaller regions, all part of the Appalachian Mountain range. Like in the Ridge and Valley Province, coal lies beneath the surface of this large region. In the northeast, the Pocono Mountains butt up against the corner of the state. The mountains range from 1,200 to 2,300 feet (366 to 700 m) high. The land is cut by many gorges, some of which have stunning waterfalls cascading to rivers deep below.

A small finger of the Blue Ridge Mountains thrusts about 50 miles (80 km) into Pennsylvania. At that point, the range dwindles to rolling hills near Gettysburg and Harrisburg.

White-water rafting in the Lehigh Gorge

The Allegheny Mountains run parallel to the Blue Ridge, extending from northern Pennsylvania to southwestern Virginia. The Alleghenies include Mount Davis, the highest point in Pennsylvania, which rises to 3,213 feet (979 m). To the western end of this region lie Pittsburgh and the Ohio River.

Central Pennsylvania is riddled with nearly 1,000 limestone caves and caverns. They are the result of underground water passing through and dissolving limestone. Lacy limestone formations hang from the cave ceilings or grow from the cave floor.

Central Lowlands

The land in the Central Lowlands slopes gently down toward the shores of Lake Erie. Erie, the largest city in the region, is a major freshwater port on the Great Lakes.

RIVERS AND LAKES

Pennsylvania has three major river systems: the Delaware, the Susquehanna, and the Ohio. The Delaware River runs the length of Pennsylvania's eastern border. The rugged surrounding land is called the Delaware Water Gap. The Lackawaxen, Lehigh, and Schuylkill rivers empty into the Delaware.

The Susquehanna River runs through east-central Pennsylvania. The West Branch and Juniata rivers feed the Susquehanna. The river basin drains 27,500 square miles (71,225 sq km), nearly half of the land area of Pennsylvania.

The Ohio River, which flows through western Pennsylvania, is the largest tributary of the Mississippi River by volume. The Allegheny and Monongahela rivers come together to form the Ohio at Pittsburgh. The Ohio has many twists and turns. Although it is naturally

Boating is popular on Glendale Lake in Prince Gallitzin State Park.

Each year, the nation awaits word from Pennsylvania to find out if Punxsutawney Phil will see his shadow on Groundhog Day.

shallow, dredging and a system of locks and dams have increased the river's depth to allow barges and ships to travel up the river to Pittsburgh and beyond.

Pennsylvania also has 4,400 smaller streams and creeks that run into the state's major rivers and fill more than 300 lakes. Conneaut Lake is the largest natural lake.

CLIMATE

In Pennsylvania, the weather changes as the elevation increases. The warmest temperatures and longest growing seasons are found in the low-lying southeast and in the west along the Ohio River valley. The coldest temperatures and most severe weather conditions are found in the central mountain regions.

Philadelphia and Pittsburgh lie at opposite ends of the state. Philadelphia's temperatures are slightly warmer, with an average high temperature in July of 86 degrees Fahrenheit (30 degrees Celsius) compared to Pittsburgh's average of 82°F (28°C). Winter temperatures tend to be colder in Pittsburgh, however, with an average January low of 18°F (–8°C) compared to an average of 22°F (–6°C) in Philadelphia. Philadelphia receives more **precipitation**—about 42 inches (107 centimeters) yearly compared to 38 inches (97 cm) in Pittsburgh. But Pittsburgh gets more snow, about 44 inches (112 cm) a year.

Lake Erie affects the weather in the Central Lowlands. The area near Lake Erie gets large amounts of snow each winter and rainfall in the summer.

Pennsylvania sometimes suffers from serious flooding. In 1889, the South Fork Dam near Johnstown burst. The floodwaters killed more than 2,200 people and destroyed the town. In 1936, warm temperatures that quickly melted snow in the mountains combined with heavy rains to produce the Great Saint Patrick's Day Flood, which devastated Pittsburgh, destroying thousands of buildings. This disaster prompted the federal government to put a flood control program in place to protect Pittsburgh. Dams were built on many of the

Weather Report

This chart shows record temperatures (high and low) for the state, as well as average temperatures (July and January) and average annual precipitation.

Record high temperature . . . . 111°F (44°C) at Phoenixville on July 10, 1936
Record low temperature . . . . –42°F (–41°C) at Smethport on January 5, 1904
Average July temperature . . . . .78°F (26°C)
Average January temperature . . . . .32°F (0°C)
Average yearly precipitation . . . . .42 inches (107 cm)

Source: National Climatic Data Center, NESDIS, NOAA, U.S. Dept. of Commerce

WORD TO KNOW

precipitation *all water that falls to the earth, including rain, sleet, hail, snow, dew, fog, or mist*

Q8 WHAT IS LAKE-EFFECT SNOW?

A8 Lake-effect snow occurs on the downwind side of the Great Lakes. It happens when cold, dry winds move across warmer masses of lake water. The air picks up water vapor, cools it, and drops the moisture as snow once the wind hits land.

Ferns cover the ground in this hemlock forest in Patterson State Park.

THE JOHNSTOWN FLOOD

On May 31, 1889, after a night of heavy rain, the South Fork Dam on the Little Conemaugh River broke. A wall of water 70 feet (21 m) high swept over Johnstown, destroying most of the town's homes, businesses, and iron- and steelmaking mills. Twenty million tons of water crashed down on the town in just 10 minutes.

rivers around the city. These dams created lakes that today are used for swimming, boating, and fishing.

PLANT LIFE

Forests cover 58 percent of Pennsylvania's land. They contain towering beeches and sugar maples. The state's trees carry a number of colorful names: black cherry, yellow poplar, white ash, silver birch, red pine, white pine, and red maple. Pennsylvania's state tree, the hemlock, provided early settlers with timber for cabins, and stands of hemlock offered protection from wind and snow. Later, the hemlock forests attracted timber companies. Leather-making companies, which made tanning chemicals from hemlock bark, also sprang up in the area.

Pennsylvania National Park Areas

This map shows some of Pennsylvania's national parks, monuments, preserves, and other areas protected by the National Park Service.

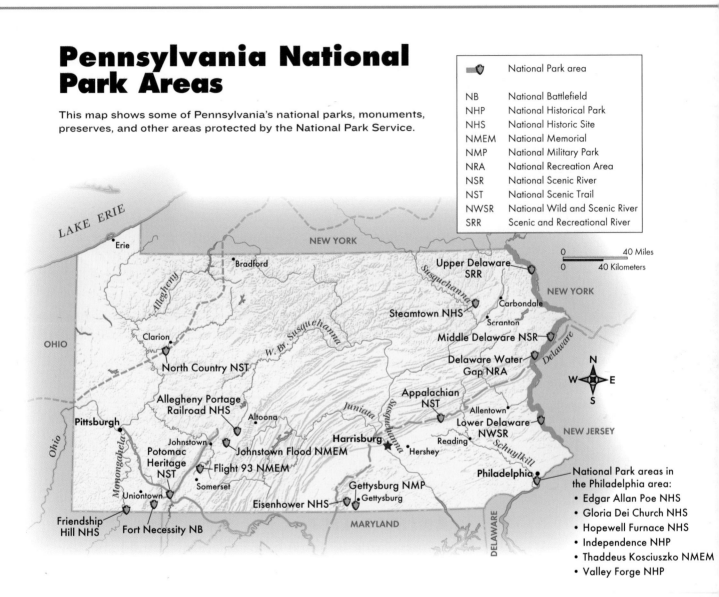

	National Park area
NB	National Battlefield
NHP	National Historical Park
NHS	National Historic Site
NMEM	National Memorial
NMP	National Military Park
NRA	National Recreation Area
NSR	National Scenic River
NST	National Scenic Trail
NWSR	National Wild and Scenic River
SRR	Scenic and Recreational River

National Park areas in the Philadelphia area:
- Edgar Allan Poe NHS
- Gloria Dei Church NHS
- Hopewell Furnace NHS
- Independence NHP
- Thaddeus Kosciuszko NMEM
- Valley Forge NHP

Native shrubs and wildflowers grace Pennsylvania's open fields and meadows, marshes, and woodlands. The state has more than 3,400 species of wildflowers and flowering shrubs. By mid-June, mountain laurel, the state flower, sprinkles the woodlands with its delicate pink tones. Azaleas, rhododendrons, dogwoods, and honeysuckles add color throughout the state. The state's

Mountain laurel

ENDANGERED SPECIES

Pennsylvania has a number of animal and plant species listed as endangered, or threatened with extinction. These include Indiana bats, which feast on insects. Other endangered animals are bog turtles, mud salamanders, and New Jersey chorus frogs. The whorled pogonia and the northeastern bulrush are two plants that are in danger.

Mud salamander

Snow geese in flight at the Middle Creek Wildlife Management Area

WORD TO KNOW

erosion *the gradual wearing away of rock or soil by physical breakdown, chemical solution, or water*

wildflowers include Dutchman's breeches, Indian pipe, spring beauty, jack-in-the-pulpit, and yellow lady's slipper. Crown vetch, the official state beautification plant, lines the state's highways, controls **erosion**, and even feeds livestock.

ANIMAL LIFE

Pennsylvania is home to a variety of animal species: 63 mammals, 159 fish, 37 reptiles, 36 amphibians, and hundreds of birds. Millions of migrating birds stop in the state on their way to winter homes in the south and summer homes in the north.

Different habitats host different species. Ponds, marshes, and bogs attract insects that use the water or reeds for laying eggs. The eastern hellbender, a type of salamander, chooses the banks of clear streams for a home, as do countless frogs and toads. The state has several different species of turtles: stinkpots, wood turtles, eastern box turtles, and map turtles, so named because of the fine yellow "map" lines on their shells. Ducks, geese, and ospreys feed in the lakes and rivers. Otters dip in the water for a swim, while beavers construct nearly indestructible lodges.

Lakes and rivers teem with muskellunge, northern pike, largemouth bass, and walleye. Fishers cast their lines along riverbanks hoping to catch brook trout, the state fish. A variety of freshwater mussels and clams lie on the bottom of lakes, rivers, and streams, feeding off tiny particles of food in the water.

Woodlands protect the state animal, the white-tailed deer. The deer share their forest homes with black bears, wildcats, foxes, minks, raccoons, skunks, squirrels, and rabbits. Peregrine falcons glide high in the air, ready to swoop down on pink-and-black crossbills,

Raccoons are among the many animals that live in Pennsylvania's forests.

RACHEL CARSON: STARTING A MOVEMENT

As a child, Rachel Carson (1907–1964) studied the ponds, springs, and meadows near her Allegheny home. Her love of nature turned into her life's work as she grew up to become a biologist and science writer. Her 1962 book, *Silent Spring*, warned people of the problems that might arise from using **pesticides**. This work sparked a worldwide environmental movement. In 1980, years after she died, Carson was awarded the Presidential Medal of Freedom.

Want to know more? See www.rachelcarson.org

WORDS TO KNOW

pesticides *any chemicals or biological agents used to kill plant or animal pests*

conservation *the act of saving or preserving something, such as a natural resource, plant, or animal species*

goldeneyes, or common grackles. Screech, barred, and great horned owls sit in their perches waiting for a careless field mouse to skitter over fallen leaves. In the meadows, bobwhite quail, ruffed grouse, and partridges build ground nests, hidden from predators by the color of their feathers.

TENDING THE ENVIRONMENT

Many industrial states have struggled with problems in the environment, and Pennsylvania has faced its share of **conservation** issues. The first state conservation action took place during the 19th century, when state officials realized that the lumber industry was rapidly destroying forests. The state set up a forestry commission to control timber harvesting and establish state forests. Today, the state government manages more than 2 million acres (809,000 hectares) of Pennsylvania forests.

Preserving clean water and air is a major concern for Pennsylvania's citizens. Many of the state's rivers became polluted by mining and industrial operations. The Schuylkill River, for example, became polluted by runoff from coal mines and sewage. Native Americans once called this river M'neyung—"the place where we drink." Controlling coal waste, adding or upgrading sewage treatment plants, and increasing water treatment returned the Schuylkill to a clean waterway.

Workers clean the shoreline of the Delaware River near Philadelphia after an oil spill in 2004.

The greatest danger faced by Pennsylvania's native plants and animals is loss of habitat. Expanding roads and new housing diminish the habitat for plants and animals. Conservation efforts have created safe homes for some of Pennsylvania's wild creatures.

CLEANING UP THE STREAMS

More than 400 miles (644 km) of Pennsylvania streams run an unhealthy yellow-red color because of pollution caused by coal mining. Pyrite is a mineral released in coal mining. When it's exposed to oxygen, it changes to a form of iron. It's carried downstream together with a dangerous substance called sulfuric acid that leaks from the mining shafts and pits. The iron and the acid create a harsh environment where hardly anything can live. Pennsylvania has a statewide project to address the problem. Federal and state laws impose fines on mining companies that contribute to this form of pollution. The laws also force companies to help clean up the existing pollution.

READ ABOUT

Early hunters used stones and spears to kill large game, such as mammoths.

13,000 BCE

The first humans arrive in what is now Pennsylvania

8000 BCE

Mammoths (above) and mastodons become extinct

8000 BCE– 1700s CE

Native people inhabit Indian Caverns

CHAPTER TWO

FIRST PEOPLE

★

SOME 15,000 YEARS AGO, HUGE MAMMOTHS AND MASTODONS LIVED IN THE LAND THAT IS NOW PENNSYLVANIA. Around this time, the first humans arrived in the region. They were hunter-gatherers, who survived by killing the large game and collecting roots, nuts, berries, and fruit. People living near the shore also collected clams and mussels.

1000 BCE
Early Woodland culture begins

1000–1500 CE ▶
People in today's Pennsylvania begin planting beans, corn, and squash together

1600s
Monongahelas become extinct

A Woodland hunter brings food home to
his family.

Grinding stone used by the Archaic
people

EARLY HUMANS

These early people were called Paleo-Indians. They
lived in caves or built rough shelters when no caves
were available.

By about 8000 BCE, the large animals such as mastodons had become extinct. People began hunting
smaller mammals, such as deer, elk, and moose, which
survive today. This was the beginning of the Archaic
period. Archaic people developed new tools such as
the atlatl, which was a spear-thrower made from a
forked stick. A spear launched from an atlatl would go
much farther than one simply thrown by hand. Archaic
people also made stone axes, knives, and other tools.

THE WOODLAND CULTURE

Around 1000 BCE, people in what is now Pennsylvania
began to plant seeds and grow crops. This development
changed the way people lived because they had more

control over their food supply. Early crops most likely included sunflowers and squash. Growing food committed these early farmers, called Woodland people, to living near their fields for long periods of time. Settled in one place, they could build larger, stronger homes. The increased food supply required better ways to store and preserve foods for later use. Woodland people began producing pottery and making baskets from reeds and grasses.

Woodland people also began building huge mounds of earth, usually cone shaped. They buried their dead in these mounds and may have also used them for other religious ceremonies. People began creating jewelry and ornaments using copper, shells, and stones. They probably traveled along rivers and overland to trade goods and crops.

NATIVE AMERICANS

Between 1000 and 1500, people created an agricultural revolution. They planted fields with three crops at the same time: beans, squash, and corn. Beans climbed the tall corn stalks, while squash provided ground cover to keep soil moist and control weeds. Beans also fed the soil by adding nitrogen that corn and squash needed to grow well.

Squash had hard skins and could be stored for the long winter. Corn could be ground into meal or flour. Beans could be eaten fresh or dried. All three produced ample seeds for planting the following year's crops. These three crops, sometimes called the Three Sisters, provided a steady supply of nutritious food. They helped the region's major cultures grow into great nations called the Monongahela, the Susquehannock, and the Lenni Lenape.

Indian Caverns, near Tyrone, served as a **Native American shelter on and off for 10,000 years**. Artifacts found there date from **8000** BCE to the **1700s** CE.

Corn, one of the Three Sisters crops

THE MONONGAHELA PEOPLE

The Monongahela people lived in today's southwestern Pennsylvania from 900 to 1600 CE. Monongahela villages and towns consisted of clusters of small houses surrounded by a wooden fence called a stockade. The stockade sometimes had a complicated entry, much like a maze, making it difficult for intruders to enter.

Between 100 and 150 people lived in a typical Monongahela village. Each family lived in a house made of a framework of wooden poles covered by slippery elm bark.

Meals were based on squash, beans, and corn. People also ate mussels, wild turkey, and meat from other animals such as squirrels, groundhogs, deer, and elk. Even if crops were plentiful, the people struggled through the winter. They called the late winter months the time of the "starving moon."

Women and children who died were buried dressed in finely embroidered and shell-decorated clothing and headgear. Men were buried with prized possessions, such as medicine pouches, pipes, and shell or stone ornaments. Graves were dug within the stockade and, for some, within the family home.

During the 1400s, both nature and other people put the Monongahela nation in peril. Monongahelas starved during several seasons of poor crops. Hunger forced Native groups to fight against one another for territory.

The Monongahela nation slowly disappeared as other Native groups moved into the region. The Monongahela people faced attacks from Senecas, Mingos, and Shawnees. By the 1600s, Monongahelas were likely extinct, although some may have joined the Iroquois people, who lived farther north.

A village of the Susquehannock people along the Susquehanna River

THE SUSQUEHANNOCK PEOPLE

Susquehannocks lived along the Susquehanna River in an area that is now Maryland, Pennsylvania, and New York. Their name means "people of the muddy water." In the 1600s, Susquehannocks were one of the most powerful nations of the mid-Atlantic. Their nation may have included 5,000 to 7,000 people divided into five groups.

The leader of each group was called a *weroance*. A weroance wore his hair long on one side and shaved on the other. He carried his arrows in a wolf-skin quiver and likely wore a bear-skin cape.

THE LENNI LENAPE PEOPLE

The Lenni Lenape people belonged to one of three clans: Wolf, Turtle, or Turkey. A son married outside his clan and went to live with his wife's clan. Children belonged to their mother's clan. Lenni Lenape commu-

LENNI LENAPE SEASONS

SEASON	MEANING
Pooxit	Time of falling leaves
Winigischuch	Time of the falling snows
Mechakhokque	When the cold makes the trees crack
Anixi gischuch	When the ground squirrels run

nities were close-knit. Members felt responsible for each other and shared food and shelter. Lenni Lenapes often lived in longhouses, large structures that housed several families.

Men, women, and children all worked for the survival of the community. Women planted and harvested the crops. They also helped butcher meat and collect fruits and nuts. They prepared foods to eat right away or to store in the clay pots or baskets they made. They wove strips of corn husks into slippers and sewed clothes from animal hides. They also wove corn husk mats for sleeping and made corn husk dolls for children to play with.

Women taught children to plant and water the crops, to harvest nuts and berries, and other jobs they would need to do as adults. Lenni Lenape boys played games to develop the skills they would need as adults, such as hunting. Races to build speed and stamina trained them to chase game and flee from enemies. Bow-and-arrow competitions developed the accuracy they would need when hunting small mammals and birds. Games such as lacrosse developed fighting skills.

Men cleared the land for crops. They hunted and fished and did most of the trading with other groups. Men made tools for farming, bows and arrows, canoes, and household items such as bowls, scoops, and ladles. They also led

Lenni Lenape village

Picture Yourself . . .

Building a Longhouse

Bad weather has destroyed one of the longhouses. Rebuilding it will be a big project, and you will need help. You begin by collecting strong, flexible limbs to serve as the framework. You strip each limb of branches and bark, stick one end into the ground, and then bend it into an arch and stick the other end in the ground. The poles are placed about 2 feet (60 cm) apart. You then tie long, straight poles horizontally across the arched poles to form a grid pattern. Once the framework is secure, you tie rush mats, sheets of bark, or skins on the framework. When you're finished, the longhouse is about 40 feet (12 m) long—big enough to house several families, their goods, sleeping mats, and food stores.

the groups. Lenni Lenapes chose their leaders based on their honesty and ability to make decisions and speeches. Elders advised the leaders in important decisions such as planting, hunting, and when to move. As winter months set in, families gathered around the fire to listen to the stories that the elders told.

Native American Peoples
(Before European Contact)

This map shows the general area of Native American peoples before European settlers arrived.

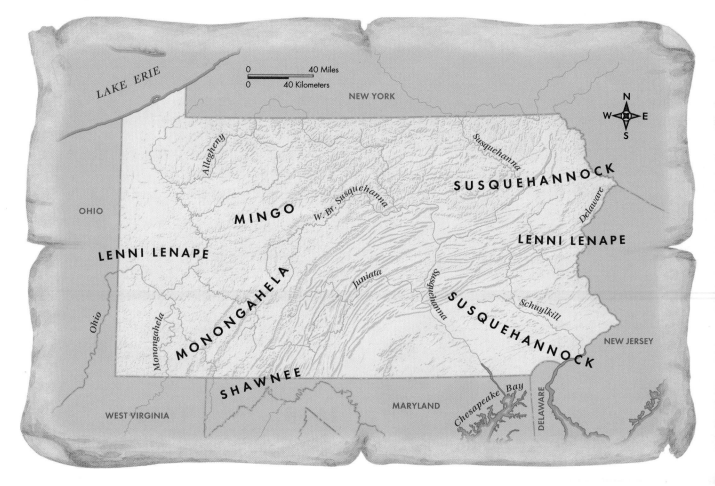

READ ABOUT

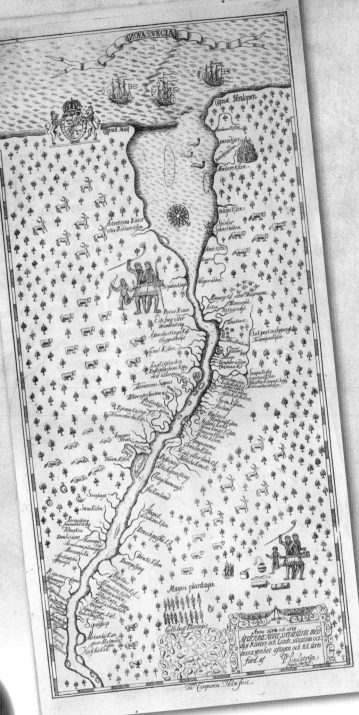

A 1655 map of the settlement known as New Sweden

1609 ▶
Henry Hudson sails into Delaware Bay

1638
New Sweden is founded

1655
The Dutch take over New Sweden

CHAPTER THREE

EXPLORATION AND SETTLEMENT

★

THE ARRIVAL OF EUROPEANS IN PENNSYLVANIA WAS NOT MARKED BY PAGEANTRY. There were no valiant soldiers marching into unknown territory. There were no triumphant military battles or conquerors planting flags of victory. Colonization here began not with a flood, but with a gentle flow of Europeans onto the land.

1682 ▶
William Penn arrives in Pennsylvania

1737
Pennsylvania Colony cheats Lenni Lenapes in the Walking Purchase

1754
The French and Indian War begins

European Exploration of Pennsylvania

This map features settlements, villages, and trading posts in the region. The colored arrow in the lower right corner shows the route that Henry Hudson took nearby in 1609.

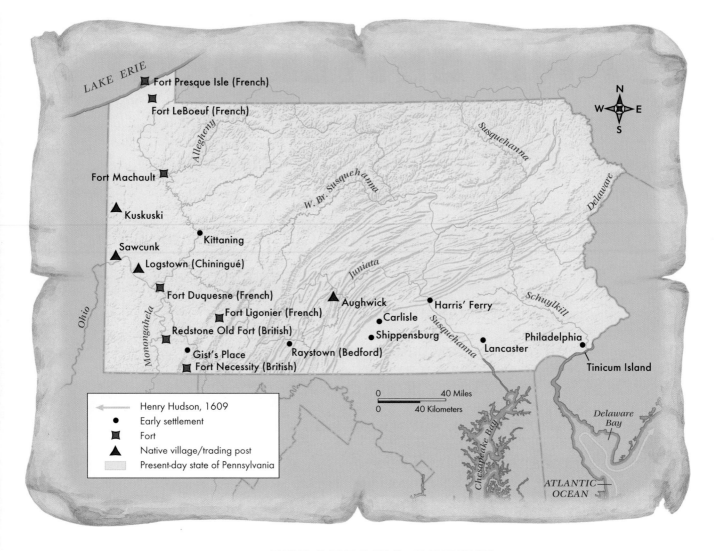

LAKE ERIE

Fort Presque Isle (French)

Fort LeBoeuf (French)

Allegheny

Susquehanna

W. Br. Susquehanna

Delaware

Fort Machault

▲ Kuskuski

● Kittaning

Sawcunk ▲

▲ Logstown (Chiningué)

Ohio

Monongahela

⬟ Fort Duquesne (French)

⬟ Fort Ligonier (French)

Redstone Old Fort (British)

● Gist's Place

⬟ Fort Necessity (British)

● Raystown (Bedford)

Juniata

▲ Aughwick

● Harris' Ferry

● Carlisle

● Shippensburg

Susquehanna

Schuylkill

● Lancaster

Philadelphia ●

Tinicum Island

N
W E
S

0   40 Miles
0   40 Kilometers

⬅ Henry Hudson, 1609
● Early settlement
⬟ Fort
▲ Native village/trading post
▢ Present-day state of Pennsylvania

Chesapeake Bay

Delaware Bay

ATLANTIC OCEAN

EUROPEANS ARRIVE

In 1609, English explorer Henry Hudson sailed his ship into Delaware Bay, took a look, and then turned around and left. Hudson was searching for a westward route to China, and he was not going to find it through

Pennsylvania. Over the next few years, several Dutch ships sailed into the area, but no one suggested founding a colony there.

In 1638, Swedish settlers established a colony called New Sweden in what is present-day Delaware. From there, they spread west toward Pennsylvania, reaching Tinicum Island near what is now Philadelphia by 1643.

The Swedish settlers were farmers, whose only interest was in growing enough wheat and rye and raising enough cattle and chickens to feed themselves. With help from enslaved Africans, they cleared the land by burning off the underbrush and killing the remaining trees.

Meanwhile, the Dutch had established a colony to the north called New Netherland. Its capital was New Amsterdam, today's New York City. By 1655, the Dutch colonists wanted to acquire land to the south. That year, they arrived in New Sweden with several hundred soldiers, and the outnumbered Swedes gave up without a fight. For the European settlers in the region, life under the Dutch was not much different from life under Swedish rule. Families farmed, grew stronger, and thrived on the land.

King Charles II

THE HOLY EXPERIMENT

In England, King Charles II faced growing problems with some of his subjects. A new Christian group had emerged, called the Society of Friends. The Friends, also known as Quakers, believe that all people are children of God and that ordinary people have spiritual light within them. They also believe that men and women have equal status before God. The Quakers refused to swear oaths to the king and the Church of England, and they believed in peace, refusing to take up arms against

MINI-BIO

WILLIAM PENN: PENNSYLVANIA'S FOUNDER

William Penn (1644–1718) was born in London, England. As a young man, Penn became a Quaker, a member of a religious society that chose simple living, peace, and following an "inner light." At Oxford University, he refused to attend required Anglican religious services and was expelled from school. His beliefs landed him in prison, where he used his time to write more religious books. Although he founded the colony of Pennsylvania, he spent a total of only four years there, 1682–1684 and 1699–1701.

? Want to know more? See http://xroads.virginia.edu/~cap/PENN/pnhome.html

WORD TO KNOW

charter *a document from a ruler granting rights to a group*

England's enemies. In the king's eyes, this was treason.

The Quakers attracted many followers, including young William Penn, son of Admiral William Penn. By age 23, the younger Penn had written a pamphlet promoting the Society of Friends, which landed him in prison. There he became more committed to his faith and began writing extensively about the Friends.

When Admiral Penn died, King Charles II owed him a great deal of money. The young Penn wanted the king to repay the debt by granting him land in North America where he could establish a colony of Quakers. The grant would relieve King Charles of two problems: the debt and the Quakers. On March 4, 1681, he signed a **charter** for a new colony west of the Delaware River. King Charles II named the land Pennsylvania, after Admiral Penn.

Penn then owned 45,000 square miles (117,000 sq km) of land. He began advertising for settlers. Penn's colony would be a Holy Experiment, a place where people could practice their religion of choice. Across Europe, members of persecuted Protestant groups thought about moving to Pennsylvania. Penn determined that Pennsylvania would be governed by its people, with a provincial council of appointed members and an assembly with elected members. The governor and his council would make the laws, and the assembly would meet to approve them.

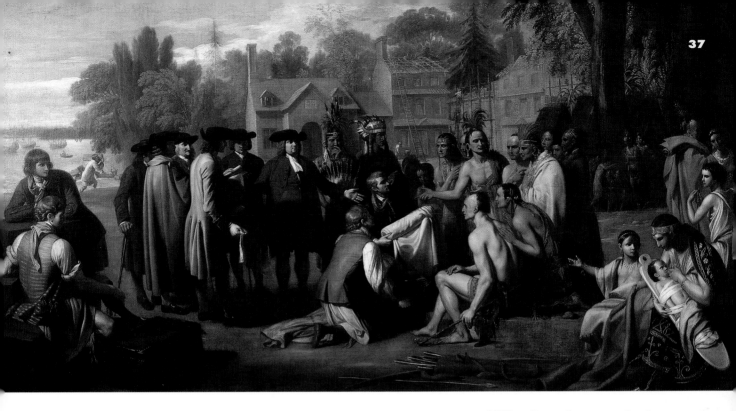

William Penn discusses a land treaty with a group of Native Americans.

In 1682, Penn and 100 colonists set sail on a ship named the *Welcome*. The trip took two months, and the travel-weary colonists suffered dearly on the ocean crossing. Many were seasick. The food was terrible. Thirty people died of smallpox on the trip, and many others were sick.

Penn's initial plans for his colony were to sell as much land as possible and to establish the city of Philadelphia. The city's plan followed a grid, with broad avenues, parks, and open spaces. Penn gave prime plots to those who had invested in his colony. Unfortunately, there were too few prime plots and too many investors claiming them. Between 1682 and 1684, 4,000 immigrants moved to Pennsylvania. Penn needed more land.

Penn met with local Lenni Lenape leaders to negotiate a peace treaty and the purchase of more land. He respected the Native people, and the Great Treaty treated the Native people fairly. (Once Penn died, though, his

Some historians claim that Penn's Great Treaty was the only treaty between white men and Native Americans that was never broken. That is not true! After Penn died, his son Thomas tricked Lenni Lenapes. The tribe lost its land and moved west in the Delaware Westward Trek.

Picture Yourself . . .

Starting a Farm in Pennsylvania

After eight weeks at sea, you finally arrive in Pennsylvania. For the first few weeks, you will be sleeping in a tent. The most important thing to do is clear the land and get crops planted. First, you burn off the undergrowth, making sure the fire does not spread. You chop down some trees and use the wood to build a house.

Now it is time to plant a crop. Your family is wealthy enough to own an ox. The beast can pull the plow, but you will have to dig up thick roots and large rocks by hand. Planting is tedious. You plunge a stick into the soil up to the 3-inch (7.6 cm) line, then drop in a seed . . . then repeat . . . and repeat . . . and repeat. Next, you haul water from a nearby stream. Every day you tend the garden and hope that it rains enough for the crops to grow so that you have food for the winter.

son and others forgot Penn's rules. They cheated Lenni Lenapes out of their land.)

Penn, however, lacked the same respect for enslaved Africans. Penn owned 12 slaves at his estate. Many Quakers opposed slavery. In 1688, four Quakers met in Germantown and issued a document protesting slavery. It was the first organized antislavery protest in history.

By 1701, Philadelphia had become an active port on the Atlantic. Fast-sailing vessels brought goods from Europe and molasses and rum from the Caribbean islands. Pennsylvania legislators had banned the slave trade in the colony, and many were increasingly opposed to enslaving people in the new free land. Quakers living in Pennsylvania pressured Penn to write a new constitution for the colony, a Charter of Privileges. The charter guaranteed religious freedom to all Pennsylvanians. Shortly after, Penn left Pennsylvania for England, never to return. He died in 1718, leaving behind the legacy of his Holy Experiment.

NATIVE AMERICANS IN THE PENNSYLVANIA COLONY

The arrival of the Europeans forever changed life for Pennsylvania's Native population. The Europeans brought with them a disease called smallpox, which devastated Native American villages. Smallpox hit the

By the mid-1700s, the harbor of Philadelphia had become a bustling port.

Susquehannocks in 1654, 1661, and again in 1677. So many Susquehannocks died of smallpox that those who remained could no longer defend themselves.

Most Susquehannocks joined the Iroquois, but several families chose to remain in Pennsylvania and live among the Lenni Lenape people. By the mid-1700s, this little group had dwindled to 20 members. They had become Christians and were living peacefully in Lancaster County. In 1763, the last remaining Susquehannocks were murdered by a group of white settlers who wanted to rid the region of all Native people. The Susquehannock way of life disappeared.

THE GROWING COLONY

By the 1720s, Philadelphia had grown into a major international port, and hundreds of ships regularly anchored in the harbor. The colony had more than

MINI-BIO

DANIEL BOONE: FRONTIERSMAN AND PATHFINDER

Daniel Boone (1734–1820) was born in southeastern Pennsylvania on a homestead established by his Quaker parents. Boone became one of the 13 colonies' first folk heroes. He was a frontiersman, hunter, trapper, and explorer. He explored the Cumberland Gap, a route through the Appalachian Mountains. He helped settle the territory of Kentucky and established the first English-speaking settlement west of the Appalachians, which was called Boonesborough.

? Want to know more?
See www.danielboonehomestead.org

40,000 residents, many of whom lived in Philadelphia.

The settlers came from various European nations. They came for religious freedom and brought their beliefs with them. Many of them were Scots-Irish, the descendants of Protestants who had moved from Scotland to Ireland in the 1600s. Other groups included Amish, Mennonites, Moravians, Pietists, Harmonists, Dutch Reformed, French Huguenots, Dunkards, the Ephrata Cloister, and Schwenkfelders. The colony also attracted a free black population.

By 1737, so many people had arrived in the colony that Pennsylvania negotiated with Lenni Lenapes to buy more land. Lenni Lenapes believed these new arrivals would deal with them as fairly as Penn had. They agreed to sell as much land as could be covered by a man walking a day and a half. Pennsylvanian James Logan hired men to run—not walk—in shifts. Lenni Lenapes were cheated out of their land, and their relationship with the colonists changed. The "Walking Purchase" allowed many more colonists to move into Pennsylvania, but the reputation for fair dealing earned by Penn was lost forever.

British settlers from eastern Pennsylvania began pushing westward. This brought them into conflict with the French, who claimed land in western Pennsylvania. The British settlers ignored that claim and settled

Many white colonists obtained land unfairly through the Walking Purchase.

there. Neither France nor Great Britain recognized Native American claims to the land. In 1754, the dispute erupted into the French and Indian War.

By the time the Treaty of Paris was signed, ending the war in 1763, both sides had serious debts from funding the long war. Great Britain won the war but struggled with the costs of maintaining an army in the colonies. The British wanted the colonists to pay the war debt, but even the most loyal colonists would bristle at paying taxes to cover the cost.

SEE IT HERE!

THE MASON-DIXON LINE

From Philadelphia's early days, Lord Baltimore, the ruler of Maryland, complained that the city was on his land. This border dispute between Pennsylvania and Maryland continued until 1763, when surveyors Charles Mason and Jeremiah Dixon determined that the border ran 15 miles (24 km) south of Philadelphia. Stones with M (for Maryland) and P (for Pennsylvania) were set at 1-mile (1.6 km) intervals. You can still see many of the original marker stones today.

READ ABOUT

An embossed
tax stamp issued
by the British
government
in 1765

1776

*The Declaration of
Independence is signed
in Philadelphia*

1780

*The Pennsylvania
legislature passes the
Act for the Gradual
Abolition of Slavery*

1787 ▲

*Pennsylvania becomes
the second state*

CHAPTER FOUR

GROWTH AND CHANGE

★

IN 1764, THE BRITISH GOVERNMENT BEGAN TAXING THE COLONIES. The Sugar Act taxed sugar and molasses. The following year, the Stamp Act required a tax stamp on every printed document—wills, newspapers, contracts, and even playing cards. The colonists' anger grew.

1859

An oil well is drilled in Titusville, starting the oil industry

1863 ▲

The Battle of Gettysburg is fought

1889

More than 2,200 people die in the Johnstown flood

Members of the First Continental Congress gather at Philadelphia's Carpenters' Hall in 1774.

WORD TO KNOW

boycott *the organized refusal to use a service or buy a product, as a form of protest*

TAXES UPON TAXES

The British eventually canceled the Stamp Act and replaced it with the Townshend Acts in 1767. These acts charged taxes on imports of lead, glass, paper, and tea. As a major trade port, Philadelphia was hard-hit by import taxes. The tax on tea affected most colonists because they drank tea with their meals.

By 1774, the colonists were so angry about British rule, taxes, and soldiers that they joined forces. The first Continental Congress met in Philadelphia at Carpenters' Hall. Representatives came from every colony except Georgia. The Congress began a **boycott** on taxed goods. They also sent George III, the British king, a letter listing their complaints.

THE AMERICAN REVOLUTION

War broke out in April 1775, when colonists exchanged fire with British soldiers in Massachusetts. The second Continental Congress met in May. They chose George Washington to command the Continental army. Thousands volunteered for service, but the army was dreadfully underfunded and poorly trained.

The soldiers needed guns and ammunition, tents and cots, food, boots, and many other supplies. Women melted down metal to make musket balls in their kitchens. They sewed uniforms, made bandages, and nursed the wounded in their homes. They contributed food to feed colonial soldiers. Some wealthy landowners and merchants provided money to support the army. Enslaved Africans labored in iron forges, where they produced tools and guns.

American soldiers trying to hold their ground at the Battle of Brandywine, 1777

WOW

At the time of the American Revolution, Philadelphia—with a population of more than 30,000—was the largest city in the colonies.

FAQ

Q8 WHY IS PENNSYLVANIA CALLED THE KEYSTONE STATE?

A8 A keystone holds the central position in a stone arch. Pennsylvania was in the center of the original 13 colonies.

SEE IT HERE!

LIBERTY BELL

Many Americans equate the Liberty Bell, on display in Liberty Bell Center, with American freedom from Great Britain. The original bell was made in 1751 and cracked the first time it rang. Although it was repaired, it sounded horrible. The bell was repaired yet again and hung in the steeple of the Pennsylvania State House in 1753. The Liberty Bell was rung for the first public reading of the Declaration of Independence on July 8, 1776.

Some colonists did not want to fight Great Britain. Some remained loyal to the king, while others simply didn't care. In 1776, patriot Thomas Paine rallied a majority of Americans to the cause of independence with the eloquent pamphlet *Common Sense*, which he wrote and published in Philadelphia. *Common Sense* was a sensation, selling hundreds of thousands of copies in less than a year. On July 4, the Declaration of Independence announced that King George III and the British government no longer had any say in governing the United States of America.

In 1777, the British set their sights on capturing Philadelphia, the temporary capital of the new nation. Victory at the Battle of Brandywine brought them closer to that goal. Washington's troops retreated behind the Schuylkill River and lost another skirmish with the British. On September 26, the British seized Philadelphia.

As the winter of 1777 set in, Washington's 10,000 troops camped at Valley Forge, north of Philadelphia. It was a difficult winter. The cabins provided little shelter, food was limited, and the weather was frigid. About 2,500 Americans died from disease and the cold. The arrival of

The Declaration of Independence was adopted by Congress in Philadelphia on July 4, 1776, but it wasn't read to the people until July 8.

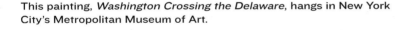

This painting, *Washington Crossing the Delaware*, hangs in New York City's Metropolitan Museum of Art.

Baron Friedrich von Steuben from Germany changed life for the soldiers at Valley Forge. Von Steuben drilled the ragtag troops until the men became true soldiers, with discipline and skills equal to British troops.

AFTER THE WAR

The war ended in 1781 with the surrender of the British at Yorktown, Virginia. Then the former colonists started to build a nation. They wrote and agreed to follow a document called the Articles of **Confederation**. This document made individual states more powerful than the national government. This caused problems for the young nation, so state representatives met in Philadelphia again in 1787. This time, they wrote the U.S. Constitution, which gave more power to the federal

FAQ

Q8 WERE THERE AFRICAN AMERICANS IN WASHINGTON'S ARMY?

A8 Yes, among the soldiers fighting in Washington's army, 5,000 were African Americans. Some crossed the Delaware River with Washington when he surprised the enemy at Trenton, New Jersey, in December 1776.

WORD TO KNOW

confederation *an association of groups that come together with common goals*

Pennsylvania: From Colony to Statehood
(1681–1787)

This map shows the original Pennsylvania Colony and the area (in yellow) that became the state of Pennsylvania in 1787.

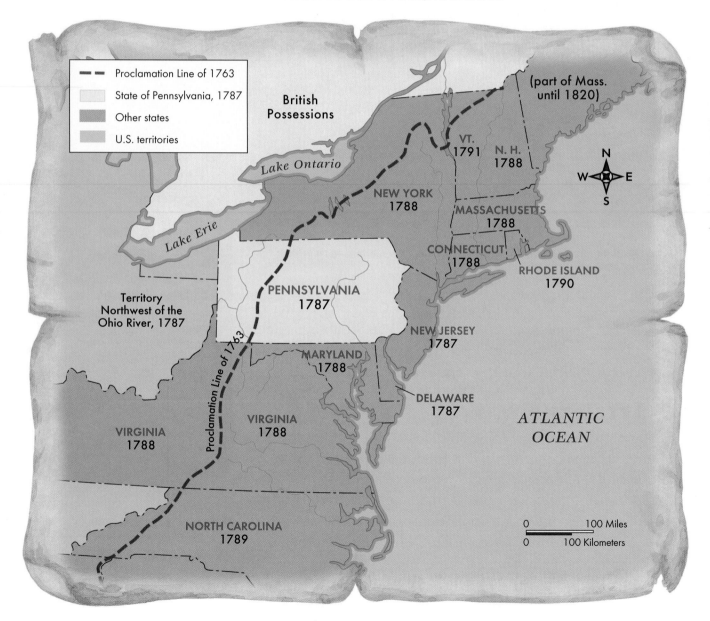

Proclamation Line of 1763
State of Pennsylvania, 1787
Other states
U.S. territories

British Possessions

(part of Mass. until 1820)

Lake Ontario

Lake Erie

VT. 1791

N. H. 1788

NEW YORK 1788

MASSACHUSETTS 1788

CONNECTICUT 1788

RHODE ISLAND 1790

Territory Northwest of the Ohio River, 1787

PENNSYLVANIA 1787

Proclamation Line of 1763

NEW JERSEY 1787

MARYLAND 1788

DELAWARE 1787

VIRGINIA 1788

VIRGINIA 1788

ATLANTIC OCEAN

NORTH CAROLINA 1789

N
W   E
S

0   100 Miles
0   100 Kilometers

government. Pennsylvania approved the Constitution on December 12, 1787, making it the second state.

George Washington became the nation's first president and took the oath of office in New York City, then the national capital. The seat of government returned to Philadelphia in 1790 for 10 years before moving again, this time to the newly built capital city, Washington, D.C.

Leaders gathered to finalize the Constitution in 1787.

SLAVERY AND FREEDOM

The number of enslaved Africans in Pennsylvania was never large. And a year before the American Revolution ended, Pennsylvania passed the Act for the Gradual Abolition of Slavery. Between 1790 and 1800, enslaved Africans in the state fell from 3,700 to 1,700. By 1840, only 64 enslaved people remained in Pennsylvania.

The oldest representative to sign the U.S. Constitution was Pennsylvania's Benjamin Franklin, who was 81 years old. Sick and weak, Franklin needed help to sign his name.

BENJAMIN FRANKLIN: SCIENTIST AND PATRIOT

Benjamin Franklin (1706–1790) was born in Massachusetts and moved to Pennsylvania, where he made his living as a printer, merchant, and author. He established the first public lending library and the first public fire department in America. Franklin was also a philosopher, politician, inventor, and diplomat. In the time leading up to the American Revolution, he rallied support for independence. He was also one of the founders of the Pennsylvania Abolition Society, the first organization in the country dedicated to ending human bondage in the land of the free.

? Want to know more? See www.pbs.org/benfranklin

Runaway slaves heading north found the North Star by following the constellation they called the Drinking Gourd, also known as the Big Dipper.

Southern states, however, had no laws to end slavery. Many enslaved people fled bondage by traveling north along what was called the Underground Railroad. These were safe places where runaway slaves were offered shelter on their route to freedom. Some who had escaped slavery stayed in Pennsylvania to establish stations on the Underground Railroad. Black churches formed, and two ministers created the Free African Society to help Africans. By 1830, Pennsylvania had become the center of the black convention movement, where people of color met every few years to protest unjust treatment, denounce slavery, and try to persuade white people to treat them as equals.

In 1826, Pennsylvania had passed a law saying that people who helped slaves escape would not be arrested and jailed for their actions. But in 1850, the U.S. Congress passed the Fugitive Slave Act, which permitted the arrest without a warrant of people suspected of being escaped slaves. This law overruled the Pennsylvania law. Under the Fugitive Slave Act, many free blacks were arrested as runaway slaves, and they were not entitled to a jury trial or to speak out on their own behalf. People helping those who were fleeing slavery could also be put in prison or fined. Southern posses rode into Northern states to capture runaways for a fee.

Despite the Fugitive Slave Act, by the 1850s free blacks had built communities in several Pennsylvania counties. Quakers and other white groups who opposed slavery and discrimination often helped. But some whites resented anyone opposed to slavery. White mobs attacked Philadelphia's black communities and even burned down Pennsylvania Hall, where antislavery meetings were held.

The executive committee of the Pennsylvania Anti-Slavery Society, 1851

WILLIAM STILL: CONDUCTOR ON THE UNDERGROUND RAILROAD

William Still (1821–1902), whose parents had been born into slavery, ran a station on the Underground Railroad in Philadelphia. He once received a wooden crate containing a runaway slave. Another time, as Still interviewed a man about his escape, he discovered that the man he was talking to was his own brother. After this, Still kept careful records of the people he helped. These records proved that he was breaking the Fugitive Slave Act, so he kept them buried in a church cemetery. After the Civil War (1861–1865), he published them as *The Underground Railroad*, the only nearly complete record of any station.

? Want to know more? See www.slaveryinamerica.org/narratives/bio_william_still.htm

MINI-BIO

ANDREW CARNEGIE: INDUSTRY TITAN

Andrew Carnegie (1835–1919) came from Scotland for a new life in the United States. Carnegie's first job was as a messenger for the Ohio Telegraph Company, where he earned $2.50 a week. Eventually he founded the Carnegie Steel Company (later part of United States Steel Corporation, today's USX) in Pittsburgh. He made millions, and used his fortune to build libraries and universities and to support world peace.

? Want to know more? See www.pbs.org/wgbh/amex/carnegie/peopleevents/pande01.html

GROWING INDUSTRY

During the second half of the 19th century, coal mining and iron and steel production pushed Pennsylvania's economy to new heights. The state had a network of roads, canals, and rail lines to transport both raw materials and finished goods. Immigrants poured into Pennsylvania from Poland and elsewhere in eastern Europe to work the mines and the mills. In 1859, Edwin Drake drilled an oil well in Titusville, Pennsylvania, starting the multibillion-dollar oil industry.

THE CIVIL WAR

In 1861, the tension between Northerners and Southerners over slavery was at a breaking point. Several Southern states withdrew from the Union and formed a

Workers at the Burpee seed processing plant in Warminster, 1800s

A recruiting poster for African American soldiers during the Civil War

new nation called the Confederate States of America. When Confederate troops fired on Union troops at Fort Sumter, in Charleston, South Carolina, on April 12, 1861, the Civil War began. Three days later, President Abraham Lincoln called out the troops in Northern states.

Black men in Pittsburgh formed the Hannibal Guards and rushed to enlist in the Union army, but Lincoln turned them down. He would not accept black recruits until 1863. He later realized his error. Without African American troops, Lincoln said in 1864, he would have had to "abandon the battlefield." They provided the Union its margin of victory.

A total of 427,286 Pennsylvanians served in the Union army and 40,002 in the navy. Of these, 8,600 were African Americans. Women served too, as nurses, cooks, and soldiers. Mary Stevens Jenkins enlisted in a Pennsylvania regiment and, disguised as a man, fought in several battles. She suffered two injuries before being sent home, yet the army never knew she was a woman.

Picture Yourself . . .

Building a Submarine

It is 1862, and you are working in a Philadelphia shipyard, finishing work on the USS *Alligator*, the Civil War's first submarine. Engineer Brutus de Villeroi designed the craft. Last week, you began installing a system to keep the air in the cabin of the submarine fresh so the crew will be able to breathe when the sub is underwater. Today, you will check all the welds along the 47-foot (14 m) length of the submarine. Could this vessel be the secret weapon the Union needs to win the war?

Pennsylvania's industries supplied the Union army. The state had iron and steel industries, shipbuilding, and factories. Pennsylvania's farm country produced ample grain, vegetables, and beef cattle, as well as dairy products.

Early in the war, the Confederate army had moved north and pushed into Pennsylvania. The first battle in the state took place on October 10, 1862, at Chambersburg. Over the next year, skirmishes caused small Union losses. But at the Battle of Gettysburg, in southern Pennsylvania, Union and Confederate troops battled fiercely for three solid days. The Union losses amounted to 3,070 killed, 14,497 wounded, and 5,434 captured or missing. Records of the Confederate losses are less accurate but estimated at 2,592 dead, 12,709 wounded, and 5,150 missing. Infection and disease killed many of the wounded long after the battle ended.

More than 40,000 soldiers were killed or wounded at the Battle of Gettysburg, which lasted three days, in July 1863.

THINK ABOUT IT!

The Gettysburg Address

Four months after the Battle of Gettysburg, President Lincoln arrived in Gettysburg to dedicate the Soldiers' National Cemetery. His Gettysburg Address is considered one of the finest speeches ever given. What do you think makes this speech impressive?

Four score and seven years ago our fathers brought forth on this continent a new nation, conceived in Liberty, and dedicated to the proposition that all men are created equal.

Now we are engaged in a great civil war, testing whether that nation, or any nation so conceived and so dedicated, can long endure. We are met on a great battlefield of that war. We have come to dedicate a portion of that field, as a final resting-place for those who here gave their lives that that nation might live. It is altogether fitting and proper that we should do this.

But, in a larger sense, we cannot dedicate—we cannot consecrate—we cannot hallow—this ground. The brave men, living and dead, who struggled here, have consecrated it, far above our poor power to add or detract. The world will little note, nor long remember what we say here, but it can never forget what they did here. It is for us the living, rather, to be dedicated here to the unfinished work which they who fought here have thus far so nobly advanced. It is rather for us to be here dedicated to the great task remaining before us—that from these honored dead we take increased devotion to that cause for which they gave the last full measure of devotion—that we here highly resolve that these dead shall not have died in vain—that this nation, under God, shall have a new birth of freedom—and that government of the people, by the people, for the people, shall not perish from the earth.

More people were killed, wounded, or captured at Gettysburg than in any other battle in the war.

The Civil War ended with the surrender of Confederate general Robert E. Lee in 1865. Soldiers returned home, many still nursing their war wounds. African Americans continued their struggle for citizenship rights. Not until 1881, after many protests and a father's lawsuit, were African American children allowed to attend a white school in Meadville. That same year, the Pennsylvania legislature voted to **integrate** all schools.

WORD TO KNOW

integrate *to end segregation and provide everyone equal access or membership*

MINI-BIO

THADDEUS STEVENS: FIGHTING FOR FREEDOM

Representative Thaddeus Stevens (1792–1868) of Lancaster was a leading figure in the Civil War. From the beginning, he urged President Lincoln to free enslaved people and arm them against the Confederacy. When the war ended, Stevens and Senator Charles Sumner urged that newly freed African Americans be granted the right to vote and be given some land of their own, to make up for centuries of their unpaid labor. Stevens and Sumner also proposed distributing the land of former slaveholders and Confederates to the poor people of both races in the Southern states.

Want to know more? See www.phmc.state.pa.us/ppet/stevens/page1.asp?secid=31

WORD TO KNOW

strikes *organized refusals to work, usually as a sign of protest about working conditions*

POSTWAR PENNSYLVANIA

The United States entered a tumultuous and violent period after the Civil War. Americans both black and white sought a fresh start on the western frontier, displacing the Native Americans who had long lived there. The federal government killed countless Native Americans in its quest for land. In 1879, Captain Richard Henry Pratt, an army officer who had fought in the Indian wars, determined that the best way to solve the so-called Indian problem would be to train Indian children in white ways. Young Indians were sent to Pennsylvania, where they attended the Carlisle Indian Industrial School.

Meanwhile, tensions were rising in the coalfields of northeastern Pennsylvania. Miners lived difficult lives. They spent much of their time underground in the muddy mines, working in low light and breathing coal dust. Workers lived in homes provided by the mining companies and shopped in mining company stores. They faced the dangers of mine cave-ins and black lung disease from breathing the coal dust.

Some miners tried to organize unions and **strikes** to improve their working conditions. Mine owners wanted to stop the unions. In one incident, after acts of violence, some of the miners were arrested. More than a dozen men were found guilty of murder or other violence. They were sentenced to hang based on the testimony of a detective hired by the mine owners. The miners swore their innocence, and many years after their executions, the detective was discredited as a liar.

In late May 1889, heavy rains led to flooding throughout south-central Pennsylvania. When the South Fork Dam on the Little Conemaugh River burst, more than 2,200 people in Johnstown drowned in the raging waters. The Johnstown flood shocked Pennsylvania and the nation. The South Fork Fishing and Hunting Club owned the dam and lake. Its members—including many of Pittsburgh's wealthiest citizens, such as Andrew Carnegie—used the lake as a summer retreat. But after purchasing the dam in 1879, the club did not adequately maintain it. It also made changes to the dam, such as lowering its height, so that two carriages could cross it at once, which weakened it. Many people blamed the club's wealthy members for the tragedy.

Despite the Civil War, coal miner strikes, racism, and the Johnstown flood, Pennsylvania thrived. As a new century dawned, the state's economy was prospering, and many people looked forward to new opportunities.

Johnstown was devastated by the flood of 1889.

58

In the early 1900s, Pittsburgh's Luna Park had thousands of visitors a day.

1915

African Americans from the South move north in the Great Migration

▲**1920**

The first commercial broadcast radio station is introduced in Pittsburgh

1941–45

Pennsylvania supplies about one-third of America's steel during World War II

CHAPTER FIVE

MORE MODERN TIMES

★

IN THE EARLY 20TH CENTURY, THE COUNTRY'S INDUSTRIAL CITIES HAD PLENTY OF JOBS. Pennsylvanians worked hard and played hard, enjoying the latest technology. Pittsburgh's citizens flocked to an amusement park called Luna Park where a night's entertainment might include riding the shoot-the-chute, a 1900's mix of a roller coaster and water ride.

1958 ►
Robert Nix is elected Pennsylvania's first African American member of Congress

1979
The incident at Three Mile Island makes Americans rethink nuclear energy

2006
WiFi Downtown Pittsburgh begins

These boys worked in a breaker, an area outside a mine where the coal is sorted and graded, for the Pennsylvania Coal Company in the 1920s.

THRIVING INDUSTRY

In the early 1900s, the steel industry was thriving. Because steel production required coal, Pennsylvania's coal mines were also busy. Industry prospered in cities from Pittsburgh to Allentown. In the late 19th and early 20th centuries, immigrants poured into Pennsylvania from Italy, Russia, Poland, and elsewhere in eastern Europe, hoping to find jobs in mines and factories.

The miners and millworkers suffered from low pay, poor health, and miserable working conditions. So they united in labor unions, fighting for better conditions and wages. John Mitchell of the United Mine Workers said, "The present miner . . . has been oppressed and ground down; but there is another generation coming up, a generation of little children prematurely doomed to the whirl of the mill and the noise and the blackness of the breaker. It is for these children that we are fighting."

World War I began in Europe in 1914. Although the United States did not join the war then, it did agree to sell materials to Great Britain and its allies. Steel mills churned out record amounts of steel for building ships, trucks, weapons, ammunition, and other goods. Farmers produced grain, vegetables, and meat, which needed to be processed for shipment to Europe. Added production in Pennsylvania meant more jobs.

As new jobs opened in the North during World War I, African Americans began leaving the rural South for the industrial cities of the North. By 1915, southern blacks were moving by the thousands in what was called the Great Migration. They hoped to build better lives than they could in the South. They were looking for better jobs, better schools, and greater freedom.

Between 1910 and 1920, the black population of Philadelphia increased by 50 percent. African Americans filled factory jobs, bought homes, and established businesses. But whites' fears about blacks settling in Philadelphia erupted in violence on July 26–29, 1918. A handful of white families attacked the homes of two African American families in their neighborhood. By the time the violence ended, three blacks and one white lay dead, and hundreds of people had been injured.

The end of World War I brought new life to an old issue: women's **suffrage**. Women had taken on traditional male roles while the men were at war, and they had proved themselves equal to the tasks. Led in Pennsylvania by Anna Elizabeth Dickinson, Lavinia Dock, Florence Kelley, and Cornelia Bryce Pinchot, groups of women marched and protested for the same voting rights as men. But early bills giving state voting rights to women went down in defeat. It was not until 1920 and the passage of the Nineteenth **Amendment** to the U.S. Constitution that Pennsylvania women could vote.

Anna Elizabeth Dickinson

WORDS TO KNOW

suffrage *the right to vote*

amendment *a change to a law or legal document*

THE GREAT DEPRESSION

The 1920s was a time of great social change. Women began wearing shorter skirts and bobbing their hair (cutting it short). They listened to jazz music and headed to the dance floor to do the Charleston or the fox-trot. In Pittsburgh, the Westinghouse Company introduced the first commercial broadcast radio station, KDKA, in 1920. On the surface, life seemed rich and exciting. In fact, steel and other industries showed lower production rates and lower profits in Pennsylvania in the 1920s.

On October 29, 1929, **stock** prices on the New York Stock Exchange plunged. Millions of dollars were lost, as the values of stocks dropped sharply. In Pennsylvania, the Philadelphia Stock Exchange suffered a similar disaster as traders put millions of shares up for sale, only to sell at huge losses.

WORD TO KNOW

stock *a share in the ownership of a company*

Waiting in an unemployment line in Pittsburgh, 1933

The stock market crash was part of the worst economic disaster the United States and the world had ever faced: the Great Depression. The Pennsylvania economy fell into a downward spiral. In Philadelphia, 50 banks failed. Individuals and businesses that had accounts at those banks lost their money. Businesses closed, putting workers out of jobs. No jobs meant no money to buy goods, pay home or farm mortgages, or even buy food. Pennsylvanians lost their homes and stood in soup lines to get free meals. Many were forced to live in ramshackle huts made of cardboard or old scrap metal. Towns of these huts were called Hoovervilles, after Herbert Hoover, the U.S. president at the time.

Citizen protests, including marches on the state capital, demanded the government take action. People of every race and religion, farmers and city workers, appealed to Governor Gifford Pinchot. He began a program of road building in rural areas to help farmers get their products to market. He proposed labor laws that made child labor illegal, offered payments to people who lost their jobs, and helped the elderly and the blind. President Franklin Roosevelt also pushed through a group of programs called the New Deal. They allowed the federal government to hire Pennsylvanians to build bridges, schools, hospitals, and libraries under

MINI-BIO

GIFFORD PINCHOT: GOVERNOR AND CONSERVATIONIST

Gifford Pinchot (1865–1946) was influential in introducing scientific forestry to the United States. As the chief of the Division of Forestry in the Department of Agriculture, which became the Forest Service, he created and preserved national parks. He also served two terms as governor of Pennsylvania. While governor, he introduced many laws to improve conservation of Pennsylvania's forests and rivers and to assist Pennsylvanians in climbing out of the Great Depression.

❓ **Want to know more?** See www.phmc.state.pa.us/ppet/pinchot/page1.asp

Crystal Bird Fauset

During World War II, Pennsylvania supplied 31 percent of America's steel and 20 percent of the steel produced throughout the world.

WORD TO KNOW

rationed *controlled the amount one could use*

the Works Progress Administration (WPA). The Civilian Conservation Corps (CCC) hired Pennsylvanians to work in state and national parks.

African Americans were among the hardest hit by joblessness during the Depression. They organized to survive economically and advance toward equality. In 1938, Philadelphia voters sent Crystal Bird Fauset to the state legislature, making her the first African American woman elected to office in the United States. She had long been a leader in the fight for equal rights in the state.

WORLD WAR II

In 1939, World War II began in Europe. Although the United States initially did not enter the war, it did provide war products to Great Britain and France. As war orders poured in, Pennsylvania went back to work. Steel plants geared up to produce even more steel than before. Shipbuilders, automobile manufacturers, weapons factories, and airplane factories all needed steel for their products. Farms produced as much food as possible, and food-processing plants went into overtime production.

After Japan bombed Pearl Harbor, Hawai'i, on December 7, 1941, the United States entered the war. Thousands of Pennsylvania men and women joined the military. As men left their jobs to serve their country, women left their homes and began working in mills and factories. And more African Americans from southern states moved north seeking better opportunities.

As part of the war effort, people across the United States planted Victory Gardens in their yards, growing their own vegetables. The government **rationed** sugar, coffee, rubber, meat, and many other products. People had ration books and could buy only as much of a rationed item as they had stamps for.

POSTWAR CHANGES

When the war ended in 1945, Pennsylvania again saw a host of changes. Many women who had worked during the war did not want to quit paid work.

Pennsylvania's steel industry declined. Resources, such as iron ore, that were needed to produce steel dwindled in Pennsylvania. Mills had to transport these resources from greater distances at greater costs. Japan, South Korea, and Brazil began producing steel more cheaply than the United States could produce it. Mills across Pennsylvania closed because they could not afford to produce steel at competitive prices. Between 1950 and 1962, Pennsylvania suffered unemployment rates 50 percent higher than the national average. The once-great steel-producing region was on its way to becoming the "rust belt."

Women joined the workforce in many factories during World War II, including the Piper Aircraft plant in Lock Haven.

BAYARD RUSTIN: CIVIL RIGHTS ACTIVIST

Bayard Rustin (1910–1987) was raised in West Chester. A Quaker, he believed in peace and dedicated his life to helping oppressed people around the world. He believed in nonviolent protests and worked closely with Martin Luther King Jr. in the fight for equal rights for African Americans. Rustin was a main organizer of the 1963 March on Washington, at which King gave his "I Have a Dream" speech.

Want to know more? See www.stanford.edu/group/King/about_king/encyclopedia/rustin_bayard.htm

In 1958, when Robert Nix was elected the state's first African American member of the U.S. Congress, racial problems were heating up in the country. Pennsylvania was making progress, but people of color were more likely than white people to be jobless, live in economically disadvantaged neighborhoods, and attend underfunded schools with untrained teachers. During the 1960s, racial tensions rose in underserved, largely minority communities in Pennsylvania's cities. In 1964, a riot broke out in the low-income African

Civil rights leader Roy Wilkins addresses a crowd in Philadelphia in 1963.

An aerial view of waste from the Hammermill Paper Company draining into Lake Erie, 1968

American neighborhoods of North Philadelphia. Rioters heard claims of police brutality against Odessa Bradford, an African American woman. More than 300 people were injured in the chaos.

While Pennsylvania wrestled with economic and racial issues, environmental problems also came to light. Rivers had become so polluted that fish could not survive, and many industrial towns suffered from severe air pollution. In the 1970s, Pennsylvanians began a serious effort to clean up their state.

In 1979, a serious problem occurred when the **reactor** overheated at the Three Mile Island nuclear power plant in Londonderry Township. No water was reaching the emergency pumps used to cool the reactor, and

WORD TO KNOW

reactor *a device for the controlled release of nuclear energy*

Members of MOVE taking a stand
against police in Philadelphia, 1978

WORDS TO KNOW

radiation *energy that is given off
in the form of waves or particles*

carcinogen *something that
causes cancer*

radiation leaked from the site. Although no lives were lost in the incident, overexposure to radiation is a known **carcinogen**. This event made many Americans rethink the idea of using nuclear power as an energy source.

TOWARD A NEW CENTURY

As the 1980s began, Pennsylvania struggled with a host of issues. In Philadelphia in 1985, neighbors reported disorderly conduct from a radical African American group called MOVE, and group members barricaded themselves in their house. The police decided to punch a hole in the roof and use tear gas to force members out. The bomb they used to make the hole caused a fire that destroyed the whole neighborhood and killed 11 people. A commission set up to investigate what had happened ruled that the mayor, the fire chief, and other top officials were "grossly negligent."

At the end of the 20th century, there was a major change in Pennsylvania's population. More than 130,000 skilled workers and their families left the state between 1995 and 2000, following the loss of jobs in western Pennsylvania. Bringing new jobs into the state became even more difficult as the availability of skilled workers decreased.

Many Pennsylvanians believe that their state's future prosperity lies in embracing high-tech opportunities and caring for the environment. The state already has 11 cyberschools, where children attend classes over the Internet. In 2006, Pittsburgh began WiFi Downtown Pittsburgh, a project that will allow citizens access to the Internet anywhere in the downtown area. Meanwhile, a comprehensive cleanup program is under way along the riverfront. Pittsburgh, once polluted and industrial, has transformed itself into a clean, modern city.

A view of modern Pittsburgh, where the Monongahela and Allegheny rivers meet to form the Ohio River

READ ABOUT

Riding a roller
coaster at
Hershey Park

CHAPTER SIX

PEOPLE

★

WHEN WILLIAM PENN FOUNDED THE PENNSYLVANIA COLONY, HE WELCOMED ALL PEOPLE, REGARDLESS OF RACE OR RELIGION. Today, the state is home to people who can trace their roots to nearly every spot on the globe. Their traditions have been woven into the fabric of Pennsylvania. From city neighborhoods to rural towns, Pennsylvanians hold on to and celebrate their culture.

Where Pennsylvanians Live

The colors on this map indicate population density throughout the state. The darker the color, the more people live there.

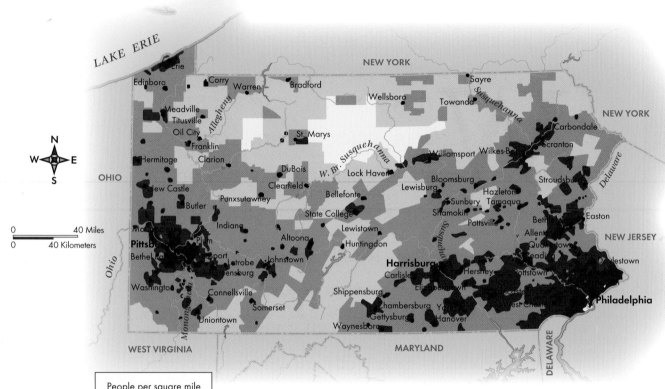

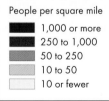

People per square mile

■	1,000 or more
■	250 to 1,000
■	50 to 250
■	10 to 50
□	10 or fewer

RURAL AND URBAN LIFE

For the past 100 years, about two-thirds of Pennsylvania's people have lived in cities. The other one-third have lived in rural areas. There were population increases of roughly 7 percent in 18 rural counties between 2000 and 2006. Most of those counties are in the eastern part of the state. Western counties, for the most part, lost population.

Philadelphia and its surrounding suburbs have grown slightly since 1990. Pittsburgh's population, how-

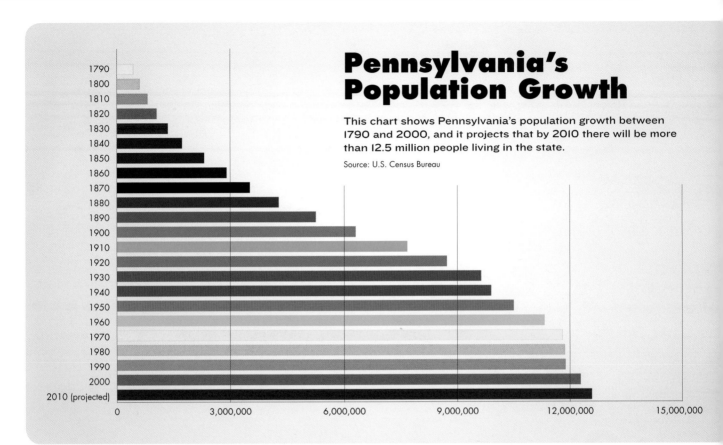

Pennsylvania's Population Growth

This chart shows Pennsylvania's population growth between 1790 and 2000, and it projects that by 2010 there will be more than 12.5 million people living in the state.

Source: U.S. Census Bureau

ever, has experienced drastic changes: since 1950, the number has fallen from about 676,000 to about 313,000. Many people moved to the suburbs but still work in the city. This has hurt the city as people take advantage of job opportunities there but no longer help pay for city services.

WHO LIVES IN PENNSYLVANIA?

The largest population groups in the state trace their heritage to Germany, Ireland, and Italy. Before the Civil War, many enslaved Africans escaped to Pennsylvania on the Underground Railroad. There, they founded a number of all-black communities, including Freedom

Big City Life

This list shows the population of Pennsylvania's biggest cities.

Philadelphia 1,448,394
Pittsburgh 312,819
Allentown 107,294
Erie 102,036
Reading 81,183

Source: U.S. Census Bureau, 2006 estimate

A dance class in Philadelphia

Q: WHAT ARE MUMMERS?

A: For the New Year's Day Mummers Parade in Philadelphia, men dress in spangles, sequins, and feathers and play banjos and saxophones. They dance down the city streets from dawn until well into the night. The term *mummer* may come from an old German word for "a disguised person." Mummers spend much of the year making their costumes and planning their parade.

Road, Africa, Hayti, and Wilmore. During the Great Migration, the African American populations grew in Chester, Philadelphia, and Pittsburgh.

The Hispanic, or Latino, population of Pennsylvania increased dramatically between 1990 and 2000 and continues to be the fastest-growing group in the state. The largest Hispanic population is found in Philadelphia, and it's largely Puerto Rican. Native Americans—including Lenni Lenapes, Cherokees, Blackfoot, Iroquois, and Sioux—account for about 15,000 Pennsylvanians. Most Pennsylvania Native Americans live in Philadelphia County.

AMISH AND MENNONITES

Pennsylvania is home to large numbers of people who belong to the Amish and Mennonite religious groups. These people typically live in very close-knit communities and maintain traditional ways. Old Order Amish call themselves "plain people." They avoid contact with the modern world as much as possible. They do not use electricity, although they may have battery-operated flashlights. They do not have radios, televisions, electric appliances, or cars. The Amish travel in horse-drawn buggies and wear plain clothes.

People QuickFacts

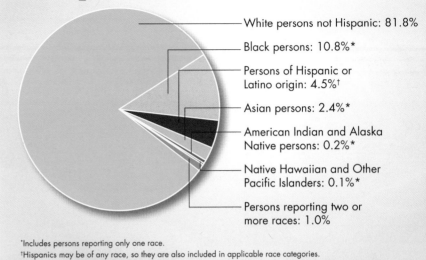

- White persons not Hispanic: 81.8%
- Black persons: 10.8%*
- Persons of Hispanic or Latino origin: 4.5%†
- Asian persons: 2.4%*
- American Indian and Alaska Native persons: 0.2%*
- Native Hawaiian and Other Pacific Islanders: 0.1%*
- Persons reporting two or more races: 1.0%

*Includes persons reporting only one race.
†Hispanics may be of any race, so they are also included in applicable race categories.
Source: U.S. Census Bureau, 2007 estimate

An Amish family traveling by horse-drawn buggy in Lancaster

An Amish teenager works on a traditional craft in Lancaster County.

Q8 WHO ARE THE PENNSYLVANIA DUTCH?

A8 People known as Pennsylvania Dutch are descendants of German immigrants who arrived in Pennsylvania before 1800. The word "Dutch" in this case comes from the German word *Deutsch*, which means "German." Amish, Mennonites, Moravians, and others are Pennsylvania Dutch.

People in the community depend on one another and work together. If a family needs a new barn, for example, everyone gathers and builds one. Amish meet for prayer in the homes or barns of congregation members.

Mennonites follow the religious teachings of Menno Simons (1496–1561), who preached that they should feed the hungry, clothe the naked, and shelter the poor. They first arrived in Pennsylvania during the 18th century. They live a simple farming life. Mennonites can wear either traditional clothes or more modern attire.

EDUCATION

The state government establishes school districts and education standards. Individual school districts have the authority to run their schools in their own way—as long as they meet state standards.

The Amish and Mennonite communities run their own schools. Amish children generally attend one-room schools that cover grades one through eight. Teachers are Amish and have, themselves, only an eighth-grade formal education. Amish parents supervise any learning beyond the eighth-grade level. Mennonite children attend religious schools. The Mennonites run elementary schools, high schools, and colleges throughout North America. Mennonite parents may also elect to send their children to public school.

Pennsylvania has more than 100 colleges and universities. The largest, Penn State, has 22 campuses, including the main campus in State College. The university's College of Earth and Mineral Sciences is highly regarded. The state's many private schools include the Ivy League's University of Pennsylvania. Carnegie Mellon, Temple, and Bucknell universities offer degrees in liberal arts and the sciences. Swarthmore, Haverford, and Bryn Mawr colleges are known for their outstanding academic programs.

On campus at the University of Pennsylvania

SEE IT HERE!

SHOPPING WITH THE PENNSYLVANIA DUTCH

Experience shopping as it was before the days of supermarkets, megamalls, and the Internet. It's Friday, and 400 local growers have brought fresh produce to the Green Dragon Farmers Market in Ephrata. Any other day, head to W. L. Zimmerman & Sons in Intercourse, and make your way up the winding stairway to the dry goods section for great bargains. In Gordonville, the Centerville Bulk Foods store sells bulk foods and candy. Don't call for directions, though. There's no phone—this is a true Amish shop.

SEE IT HERE!

PAT'S KING OF STEAKS

At the intersection of Ninth and Wharton in Philadelphia, the original Pat's King of Steaks is still grilling Philly cheesesteaks for its patrons. During the Great Depression (1929–41), owner Pat Olivieri was sick of eating hot dogs at his hot dog stand. He wanted a steak! His brother bought a small piece of steak from the local butcher. Olivieri sliced it thin, added onions, fried up the lot, and piled it onto a piece of Italian bread. Later Olivieri added cheese to the sandwiches. Voilà! The Philly cheesesteak was born.

Fresh produce for sale at a farmers' market in Pennsylvania Dutch Country

HOW TO TALK LIKE A PENNSYLVANIAN

The Pennsylvania Dutch have added some colorful phrases to the local language. Here are a handful of sayings:

Get'n to wet'n	Looks like rain soon.
Stop being so shussly	Must you keep tripping over your own feet?
Outen the lights	Turn off the lights.
You are fressing	You are indulging your sweet tooth, eating candy.
Tastes like more	May I please have a second helping?

HOW TO EAT LIKE A PENNSYLVANIAN

From Heinz pickles in Pittsburgh to shoofly pie in the eastern part of the state, Pennsylvania is a food lover's delight. Over the centuries the state's many immigrants brought with them a rich heritage of foods. Across the state, Pennsylvanians can dine on Polish, German, and Italian dishes, and fresh produce is plentiful. Chicken and dumplings, a Pennsylvania Dutch tradition, will have people saying, "Tastes like more!"

MENU

WHAT'S ON THE MENU IN PENNSYLVANIA?

★ ★ ★

Philly cheesesteak

Philly cheesesteak

Thinly sliced steak, fried with onions, topped with provolone cheese, and served on Italian bread

Lebanon sausage

A bologna-like sausage that is sliced and served on a sandwich

Pierogi

Stuffed dumplings—served in every Polish neighborhood—typically filled with cabbage, potatoes, cheese, or mushrooms

Sauerkraut

Pickled cabbage cooked with caraway seeds and served with pork

Scrapple

Cornmeal and sausage mush, often baked in a loaf, then sliced and fried.

Shoofly pie

TRY THIS RECIPE
Shoofly Pie

"I Break for Shoofly Pie" is the official bumper sticker of Pennsylvania. This molasses pie has a "wet" bottom and a dry, crunchy top. Have an adult help you with this recipe.

Ingredients:
1 cup all-purpose flour
½ cup packed light brown sugar
1 teaspoon ground cinnamon
½ teaspoon nutmeg
¼ teaspoon plus a pinch of salt
6 tablespoons cold unsalted butter,
    cut into ½-inch pieces
1 cup boiling water
½ cup molasses
½ cup light corn syrup
1 teaspoon baking soda
1 large egg, lightly beaten
1 frozen pie crust

Instructions:
1. Preheat the oven to 325°.
2. To make the topping, combine the flour, brown sugar, cinnamon, nutmeg, and ¼ teaspoon salt in a medium bowl. Work in the butter with the tines of a fork until the mixture turns into fine crumbs. Set this bowl aside.
3. To make the filling, stir together the boiling water, molasses, and corn syrup in another medium bowl. Whisk in the baking soda, egg, and a pinch of salt.
4. Pour the molasses mixture into the frozen pie crust. Scatter the crumb topping on top.
5. Place the pie on a cookie sheet. Bake for about 50 minutes, or until the filling is set and the top is golden brown. Cool for 30 minutes.

Painter Horace Pippin in West Chester, 1945

THE HEX!

Hex signs are folk art, fantasy, and decoration. They are beautifully painted, hexagonal (six-sided) patterns painted on Pennsylvania Dutch barns. Hex signs may feature stars, hearts, birds, and tulips. What do they mean? Some believe they are symbols to ward off witches, but most say that hex signs have no relation to magic. They are simply six-sided decorations.

ARTS

Across the state, artists produce baskets, needlework, stained glass, pottery, weavings, and many other crafts. Amish women sew fine quilts, while Amish men craft simple, elegant furniture. Craft fairs feature a variety of homemade artworks, as well as jams, jellies, and pickles.

Pennsylvanians have contributed to every major art movement of the 20th century. Painter Horace Pippin depicted the West Chester community where he lived. Philadelphia's Laura Wheeler Waring became known for her accurate portraits of African Americans, including opera singer Marian Anderson. Waring trained at the Pennsylvania Academy of Fine Arts.

The Wyeths from Chadds Ford, near the Delaware border, have produced three generations of accomplished artists. N. C. Wyeth (1882–1945) illustrated classic books such as *Treasure Island, The Yearling, Robinson Crusoe,* and *The Last of the Mohicans.* His son Andrew (1917–) paints realistic portrayals of people and landscapes. Jamie Wyeth (1946–), Andrew's son, also paints realistic landscapes and portraits.

Modern art by Pennsylvanians covers a wide range of media. A sculpture by Alexander Calder graces Philadelphia's City Hall. Andy Warhol began his career as an illustrator and became famous for his paintings and prints of everyday objects, such as a Campbell's soup can and a box of Brillo pads.

MINI-BIO

MARY CASSATT: IMPRESSIONIST ARTIST

Mary Cassatt (1844–1926), who was born in Allegheny City, became a painter and printmaker who lived much of her life in Paris, France. She was a member of the impressionist movement. Painters in this style were more concerned with capturing light and shadow than with realism. Cassatt's favorite subjects were mothers and children and the social lives of women. One of her best-known works is *The Child's Bath*, painted in 1893.

❓ **Want to know more?** See www.metmuseum. org/explore/CASSATT/HTML/index.html

MUSIC

American popular music emerged in the 1800s, when Lawrenceville's Stephen Foster got toes tapping and tears dropping to tunes such as "Camptown Races" and "Old Folks at Home." Foster is known as the Father of American Music. A century later, two brothers from Shenandoah became big-name big band leaders. Jimmy and Tommy Dorsey drew people to the dance floor to do the fox-trot, the jitterbug, and the Lindy Hop. Meanwhile, singer Marian Anderson wowed audiences around the world with her exquisite voice.

Pennsylvanian Chubby Checker (center) joins Dick Clark (right) and singer Conway Twitty in dancing the twist in 1960.

MINI-BIO

MARIAN ANDERSON: WORLD-CLASS SINGER

Classical singer Marian Anderson (1897–1993) grew up in Philadelphia. By the late 1920s, she had performed at the top concert halls of New York City. But in 1939, she was refused permission to sing at Constitution Hall in Washington, D.C., because she was black. People across the nation were shocked. First Lady Eleanor Roosevelt persuaded Secretary of the Interior Harold Ickes to invite Anderson to sing at the Lincoln Memorial. Mrs. Roosevelt was among a crowd of 75,000 who attended the outdoor concert. Anderson was the first African American to perform with the New York Metropolitan Opera.

❓ **Want to know more?** See www.lkwdpl.org/wihohio/ande-mar.htm

Rock-and-roll music got a boost in 1956 with Dick Clark's TV show *American Bandstand*. Many performers got their start on Clark's show, including Pennsylvanians Chubby Checker (inventor of the twist) and Patti LaBelle and the Bluebells. Pennsylvania musicians really came into their own in the 1970s, when the style called Philly Soul filled the radio airwaves with tunes from the O'Jays and Teddy Pendergrass.

LITERATURE

Keystone State novelists and poets made their mark in the 1800s. Edgar Allan Poe penned several of his eerier works while living in Philadelphia. "The Raven," "The Gold-Bug," and "The Murders in the Rue Morgue" were written in Pennsylvania. Novelist Conrad Richter portrayed frontier life in *The Trees, The Fields,* and *The Town.*

Many Pennsylvania writers have had an impact on social issues. W. E. B. DuBois wrote *The Philadelphia Negro: A Social Study* in 1899. Author Mary Roberts Rinehart exposed the challenges of being a housewife in a Pennsylvania German community. Nobel Prize–winner Pearl S. Buck revealed the lives of the Chinese in *The Good Earth.* Perhaps the books that had the greatest social impact were *The Sea Around Us* and *Silent Spring* by Rachel Carson. These books helped launch the conservation movement of the late 20th century.

Pennsylvania can claim many authors whose characters have entertained children in bedtime stories and chapter books, such as Lloyd Alexander's knights and dragons, Kate DiCamillo's brave mouse Despereaux, and E. L. Konigsburg's Mrs. Basil E. Frankweiler.

NEWBERY-WINNING AUTHOR

Elaine Lobl Konigsburg (1930–) was born in New York and grew up in the small towns of Phoenixville and Farrell, Pennsylvania. She loved reading as a child, but she didn't find her life in Pennsylvania reflected in the books she read. As a writer, she has filled her books with kids like her—smart, curious, sometimes difficult kids from the city and suburbs. Konigsburg's books include *From the Mixed-up Files of Mrs. Basil E. Frankweiler,* about a brother and sister who run away from home and hide in New York City's Metropolitan Museum of Art. She has twice won the Newbery Medal for the year's outstanding American children's book.

MINI-BIO

WILT CHAMBERLAIN: BASKETBALL ALL-STAR

One of the National Basketball Association's all-time most dominant players, Wilt Chamberlain (1936–1999), came from Philadelphia. At 7 feet 1 inch (216 cm) tall, he was called Wilt the Stilt. He dominated the game, setting record after record in scoring and rebounding. He is the only player to date to score more than 100 points in a single NBA game. Chamberlain was elected to the Naismith Memorial Basketball Hall of Fame in 1978.

? Want to know more? See www.hoophall.com/halloffamers/bhof-wilt-chamberlain.html

SPORTS

For many Pennsylvanians, the ideal autumn weekend is filled with football. Friday night is high school football, followed by college games on Saturday and the pros on Sunday when Pennsylvania fans cheer on the Eagles (Philadelphia) or the Steelers (Pittsburgh). Football has a long history in Pennsylvania. The first professional football team

Pittsburgh Steelers quarterback Ben Roethlisberger dives into the end zone during the team's Super Bowl win in February 2006.

in Pittsburgh took the field in 1892, followed by the Philadelphia Professionals in 1901.

In addition to football, Pennsylvania sports fans support the state's basketball, baseball, and hockey teams. In hoops, the Philadelphia 76ers were National Basketball Association (NBA) champs in 1967 and 1983. On the diamond, baseball fans cheer or boo the Pittsburgh Pirates or the Philadelphia Phillies. At the rink, hockey fans have a lot to cheer for. The Pittsburgh Penguins were Stanley Cup champs in 1991 and 1992 and Eastern Conference Champs in 2008. The Philadelphia Flyers won the cup in 1975.

Youth sports programs abound in Pennsylvania. From courts to fields to rinks to slopes to pools, there's something fun for everybody year-round.

MINI-BIO

JIM THORPE: GREATEST ATHLETE IN THE WORLD

Born in Oklahoma, Jim Thorpe (1887–1953) belonged to the Sauk tribe to whom he was known as Wa-Tho-Huk (Bright Path). Thorpe moved to Pennsylvania in 1904 to attend the Carlisle Indian Industrial School. In 1912, he won both the Olympic decathlon and pentathlon, although his medals were later taken away because he had once been paid to play a baseball game. At the time, Olympic athletes were not allowed to be paid for any sporting competition. Thorpe also had two successful professional sports careers. He played baseball for the New York Giants and the Cincinnati Reds, and then played football for the Canton Bulldogs and the Cleveland Indians.

❓ **Want to know more?** See www.profootballhof. com/hof/member.jsp?player_id=213

The first-ever World Series game was played in Pittsburgh in 1903. The Pirates won the first game 7–3 against the Boston Americans, but the Americans won the series.

Q: WHAT IS THE SCHUYLKILL NAVY?

A: Many of the United States's most prominent rowers are part of the Schuylkill Navy—rowers who haul out their boats, called sculls, and oars to practice on the Schuylkill River. At least one oarsman from the boathouses on the Schuylkill has been on the U.S. Olympic rowing team since the first Olympics in 1896.

READ ABOUT

Lawmakers and students watch as Governor Edward Rendell signs the state budget in 2007.

CHAPTER SEVEN

GOVERNMENT

★

ORIGINALLY, WILLIAM PENN'S COLONY WAS CALLED THE QUAKER COMMONWEALTH. The word *commonwealth* is a synonym for "state" and refers to a government that works for the good of its people. Pennsylvania is one of four states that chose to be considered a commonwealth. The other three are Kentucky, Massachusetts, and Virginia. Since colonial days, Pennsylvania has had a representative government.

The state capitol in Harrisburg

THE CENTER OF GOVERNMENT

Harrisburg did not become the capital until 1812. The city was chosen because of its central location and connection to transportation routes. Since the early 1800s, Harrisburg has played a vital role in riverboat traffic in Pennsylvania. Lying on the banks of the Susquehanna River, Harrisburg was a focal point in the development of the Pennsylvania canal system and a railroad hub. The city was named for John Harris, a ferry operator who set out the plan for the town in 1785. It was Harris who donated land for the capitol.

The state capitol complex houses many of the state's agencies and departments. The main offices of the governor, the state general assembly, and the state supreme court are located in the capitol. The departments of finance, transportation and safety, health and welfare, and labor and industry are in buildings near the capitol.

Capitol Facts

Here are some fascinating facts about Pennsylvania's state capitol.

- The dome rises 272 feet (83 m) high and weighs 52 million pounds (24 million kilograms).
- The central staircase is modeled on one in the Paris Opera House.
- The rotunda design is based on St. Peter's Basilica in Rome, Italy.
- Construction was completed in 1906.
- Construction materials include Vermont granite, glazed terra-cotta tiles, gold leaf, and stained glass.
- Edwin Austin Abbey created the *Reading of the Declaration of Independence* mural for the house of representatives, which was completed by his student Ernest Board because Abbey was ill.
- Violet Oakley painted 43 murals for the capitol, including *Unity* for the senate chamber.
- A series of tile images in the floor, created by artist Henry Mercer, depicts the history of Pennsylvania from prehistoric times.

Capital City

This map shows places of interest in Harrisburg, Pennsylvania's capital city.

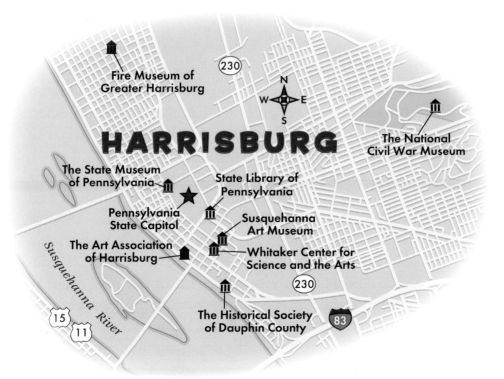

WORD TO KNOW

revenue *the money a government receives through taxes and other sources*

THE EXECUTIVE BRANCH

The executive branch of Pennsylvania's government consists of the governor, the lieutenant governor, the attorney general, the auditor general, the state treasurer, and the secretary of education. The governor heads up the state government. Other members of the executive branch report to the governor.

The governor and lieutenant governor run for office at the same time and are limited to two consecutive four-year terms. In the event that the governor is unable to fulfill his or her duties, the lieutenant governor takes over as governor.

The governor's primary responsibility is enforcing Pennsylvania's laws. The governor has a cabinet of advisers to help with managing the government. These advisers deal with areas of particular interest to the state, such as banking, education, insurance, agriculture, labor and industry, health, and public welfare. The department of **revenue** collects taxes, and the state treasurer oversees the spending of state funds. Under the governor, the state police investigate and enforce state laws, while the corrections department oversees prisons. In addition to these areas, the governor has the power to pardon people convicted of crimes and serves as commander in chief of the state's national guard.

In 2003, Governor Edward Rendell created a new commission, the Governor's Cabinet on Children and Families, to streamline children's services. One of the first programs to come from the commission is a plan for improving the health of Pennsylvania's children. The plan mixes safety, nutrition, and exercise programs and addresses the growing problem of overweight children. The program includes health education in schools through the department of education.

Pennsylvania State Government

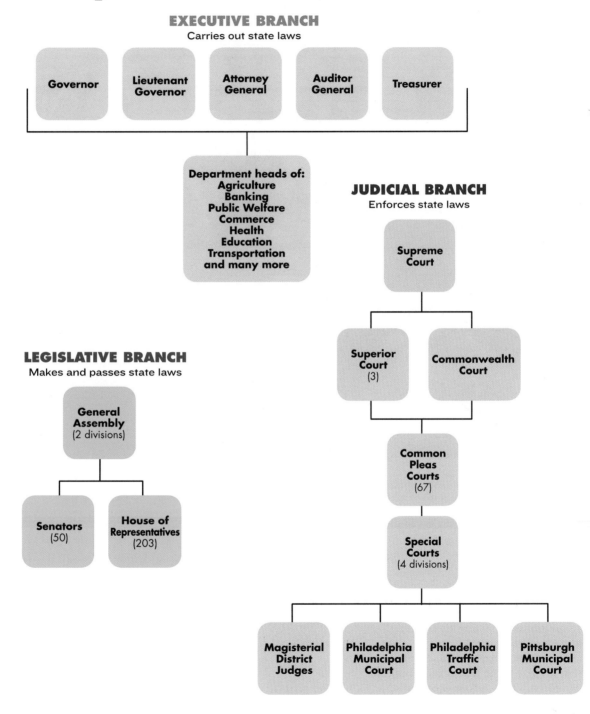

EXECUTIVE BRANCH
Carries out state laws

Governor

Lieutenant Governor

Attorney General

Auditor General

Treasurer

Department heads of:
Agriculture
Banking
Public Welfare
Commerce
Health
Education
Transportation
and many more

JUDICIAL BRANCH
Enforces state laws

Supreme Court

Superior Court (3)

Commonwealth Court

Common Pleas Courts (67)

Special Courts (4 divisions)

Magisterial District Judges

Philadelphia Municipal Court

Philadelphia Traffic Court

Pittsburgh Municipal Court

LEGISLATIVE BRANCH
Makes and passes state laws

General Assembly (2 divisions)

Senators (50)

House of Representatives (203)

Members of the Pennsylvania House of Representatives take the oath of office in January 2007.

The Pennsylvania House of Representatives is lit by six chandeliers and a total of more than 1,000 lightbulbs. Each of the larger light fixtures weighs more than an adult elephant.

THE LEGISLATIVE BRANCH

The legislative body of Pennsylvania is the General Assembly, which comprises the senate and the house of representatives. The senate has 50 members, and the house has 203 members.

Senators run for election every four years. Only half of the senate runs for office at a time, which ensures that there are some experienced senators serving at all times. Potential senators must be 25 years old and live in their districts for at least one year prior to the election. To become a member of the house of representatives, a person must be at least 21 years old and have lived in his or her district for at least a year. Members of the house run for election every two years.

All laws in Pennsylvania begin in either the house of representatives or the senate. A bill is presented as an idea and sent to a committee for further study. A bill about textbooks would be sent to the committee on education, for example. If the committee agrees that the bill should be law, it presents the bill for discussion. A bill must be passed by both the senate and the house before it can be sent to the governor to be signed into law. Only the house of representatives can introduce a bill dealing with taxes.

WACKY LAWS IN PENNSYLVANIA

Pennsylvania has some pretty wacky old laws lingering on the books. Do you think any of these are still enforced?

- Any motorist who sights a team of horses coming toward him must pull well off the road, cover his car with a blanket or canvas that blends with the countryside, and let the horses pass. If the horses appear to be skittish, the motorist must take his car apart piece by piece and hide it under the nearest bushes.
- In Morrisville, women need a permit to wear cosmetics.
- A person is not eligible to become governor in Pennsylvania if he or she has participated in a duel.
- In Philadelphia, you can't put pretzels in bags, based on the Act of 1760.

Representing Pennsylvania

This list shows the number of elected officials who represent Pennsylvania, both on the state and national levels.

OFFICE	NUMBER	LENGTH OF TERM
State senators	50	4 years
State representatives	203	2 years
U.S. senators	2	6 years
U.S. representatives	19	2 years
Presidential electors	21	—

FAQ

Q: WHAT EXACTLY IS THE MACE?

A: The history of the mace goes back to early Roman times. It was a bundle of wooden rods bound together by a red strip of leather, with an ax blade at the top. Roman officers carried the mace ahead of judges and emperors to show their authority. Today, the Pennsylvania Senate and House of Representatives each have a mace to show the authority of the senate president or the speaker of the house.

JAMES BUCHANAN: PENNSYLVANIA'S ONLY PRESIDENT

James Buchanan (1791–1868) was born in Mercersburg, in the southern part of the state. He became a lawyer and then entered politics, serving in the U.S. House and Senate and as secretary of state before becoming the 15th president. Buchanan, who was the only U.S. president to never marry, is often ranked as one of the worst presidents in American history because he did not act to prevent the Civil War.

? Want to know more? See www.whitehouse.gov/history/presidents/jb15.html

THE JUDICIAL BRANCH

The state's judicial branch is divided into 60 districts. Courts hear trials that are criminal or civil. A criminal case deals with a crime such as murder or theft. A civil case deals with a dispute, such as failure to fulfill a legal contract or a lawsuit over personal injury.

Different levels of courts deal with different legal problems. Children who commit crimes are tried in juvenile court. Issues of divorce, child custody, adoption, wills, and deeds are heard in the court of common pleas. The superior court hears serious criminal cases as well as appeals from the court of common pleas regarding children and their families. The commonwealth court hears civil cases and appeals from state agencies resulting from decisions in the court of common pleas.

The superior court consists of a president judge and 14 commissioned judges, all elected by the people. Superior court judges sit in panels of three judges, with assistance from a senior judge who has been appointed by the state supreme court. The commonwealth court also has a president judge. There are eight other judges who sit on the commonwealth court. They, too, are assisted by senior judges appointed to the position.

The highest court is the Pennsylvania Supreme Court. This court has six justices and a chief justice. The supreme court hears appeals from the superior and commonwealth courts. The justices may also hear appeals from the court of common pleas, specifically in cases dealing with the death penalty. The decision made by the supreme court is final, although cases may be appealed to the U.S. Supreme Court.

Pennsylvania Counties

This map shows the 67 counties in Pennsylvania. Harrisburg, the state capital, is indicated with a star.

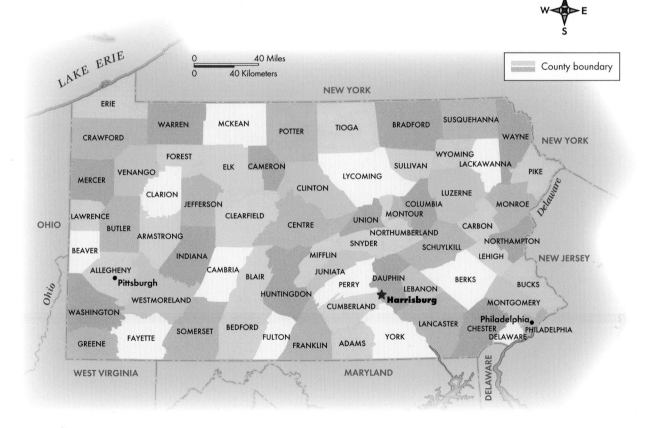

State Flag

In 1799, the General Assembly approved the official Pennsylvania flag. The design includes two draft horses, a scroll that reads, "Virtue, Liberty, and Independence," and a multicolored coat of arms against a dark blue field. The blue in the flag matches the blue in the U.S. flag.

State Seal

The General Assembly approved the state seal in 1791. The face of the seal shows a crest with a ship under full sail, which represents commerce; a plow, which represents rich natural resources; and three bundles of wheat, which represent agriculture. The corn on the left represents the state's past, and the olive branch on the right represents the hope of a peaceful future. A bald eagle, the symbol of the United States, stands atop the crest. The reverse side pictures Liberty (a woman) dominating Tyranny (a lion), along with the statement "Both Can't Survive."

READ ABOUT

A tugboat guides a cargo ship along the Delaware River near the Philadelphia harbor.

CHAPTER EIGHT

ECONOMY

★

P ENNSYLVANIA'S STATE ECONOMY IS STRONG, RANKING SEVENTH IN THE NATION. It balances agriculture and industry, with support from services and transportation. The state's central location on the East Coast provides an abundance of transportation options, including major airports in Philadelphia and Pittsburgh. A network of highways connects all areas of the state, while the ports of Erie and Philadelphia provide access by water. The port of Philadelphia welcomes container-ships from around the world.

A worker harvests pears on a farm in Biglerville.

Q8 WHAT ARE SOME OF PENNSYLVANIA'S UNUSUAL FARM PRODUCTS?

A8 Pennsylvania produces about 66,000 gallons (250,000 liters) of maple syrup each year. The state's farms also produce honey, trout, and mink pelts. Mink pelts bring in the most money per unit, but trout farming is the largest of these agribusiness industries, amounting to $4.8 million yearly.

AGRICULTURE

Livestock and livestock products generate nearly 70 percent of the state's agricultural dollars. Dairy farms dot the northeast and northwest, producing milk, butter, cream, ice cream, and cheese. Beef cattle, broiler chickens, and eggs add significantly to the agricultural market. The state produces more than 10 billion pounds (450 million kg) of milk and milk products and 6.6 billion eggs yearly.

The state grows greenhouse and nursery products, mushrooms, corn for grain, hay, and soybeans. Nine percent of agricultural income comes from greenhouse products, including bedding flowers, herbs, vegetable seedlings, young trees, and shrubs. Mushrooms, a major product in Pennsylvania, account for 8 percent of agricultural dollars. Corn is grown to make corn syrup, cornmeal, and cattle feed. Other grains include hay, alfalfa, oats, and sorghum. Soybeans provide oil, tofu, biodiesel fuel, insulation, adhesives, and soy-based candles.

Many farms grow vegetables, sold commercially or through farmers' markets. Sweet corn brings the highest revenue, followed by tomatoes, strawberries, and pumpkins. Sweet corn and snap beans are also processed as frozen and canned foods. Pennsylvania orchards produce tons of grapes and peaches, 515 million pounds (234 million kg) of apples, and more than 2.6 million pounds (1.2 million kg) of tart cherries.

Tomatoes

MANUFACTURING AND INDUSTRY

Pennsylvania ranks seventh among states in manufacturing output. The top manufactured products in the state are chemicals. The leading makers of prescription drugs and aspirin are located in Pennsylvania. Other chemical products made in Pennsylvania include paint, **petrochemicals**, and **synthetic** resins. Petrochemicals are used to make plastics, synthetic rubber, and fibers. Synthetic resins are used in making soap and glue and in purifying water.

Processed food plants provide jobs for thousands of Pennsylvania citizens. Pittsburgh is the home of Heinz, a maker of pickles, soups, and the most popular ketchup in the nation. Hershey is the nation's chocolate capital. Even the city's streetlights are shaped like Hershey's Kisses. The state is a leader in canning mushrooms,

WORDS TO KNOW

petrochemicals *chemicals produced from oil or natural gas*

synthetic *related to something that doesn't occur in nature*

Top Products

Agriculture Milk, beef cattle, broilers, eggs, greenhouse and nursery products, mushrooms, corn, hay, soybeans, sweet corn, tomatoes, strawberries

Manufacturing Chemicals, medicines, paint, petrochemicals, synthetic resins, processed foods, computer and electronics equipment, scientific instruments

Mining Coal, limestone, natural gas, sand and gravel, petroleum

Q8 WHAT CAN YOU MAKE FROM A BARREL OF PENNSYLVANIA CRUDE OIL?

A8 The Drake Well Museum claims that a barrel of oil can produce all of the following products:

- 280 miles (450 km) worth of gas for a medium-sized car
- 40 miles (64 km) worth of diesel for a truck
- 70 kilowatt hours of electricity
- 750 plastic combs
- 540 toothbrushes
- 170 birthday candles

Plus: plastic dustpans and drinking cups, polyester shirts, hula hoops, crayons, tar, engine oil, jet fuel, and solvents

producing sausage, and processing potato chips and pretzels.

The third most valuable manufacturing industry produces computers, electronics, and communications equipment.

MINING

Pennsylvania is the only place in the United States where anthracite coal is mined and one of several states extracting bituminous coal. The most common use for anthracite coal is in home furnaces. The coal burns cleanly with very little soot. Because it is so hard and clean burning, anthracite coal is expensive. Bituminous coal is also hard coal but of poorer quality than anthracite coal. Bituminous coal is used in making coke. Coke is made by heating bituminous coal in an oven to remove its impurities. The coke is used as a fuel in making iron and steel.

Pennsylvania has extensive coal reserves, but companies also gather coal from the waste piles of old mines. They also collect coal by bank mining, a form of mining coal from the surface. Pennsylvania's coal production in 2005 amounted to just over 68 million tons.

Major Agricultural and Mining Products

This map shows where Pennsylvania's major agricultural and mining products come from. See a cart full of coal? That means coal is found there.

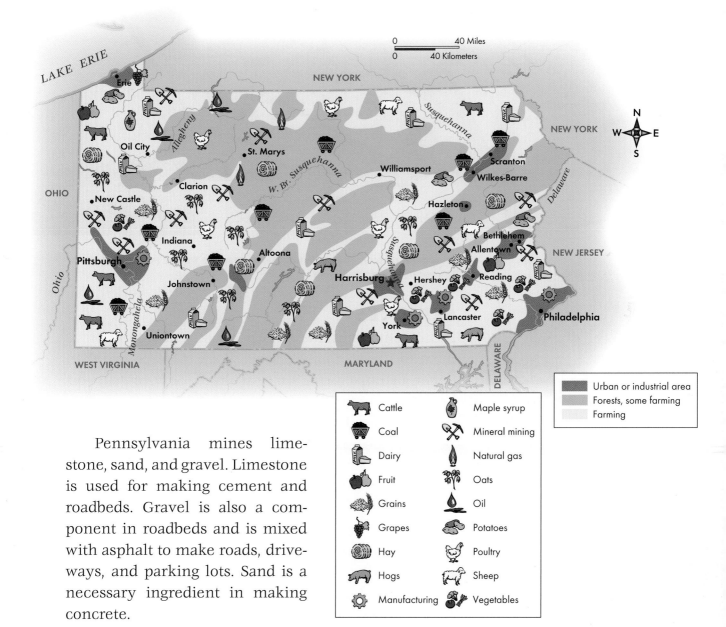

Pennsylvania mines limestone, sand, and gravel. Limestone is used for making cement and roadbeds. Gravel is also a component in roadbeds and is mixed with asphalt to make roads, driveways, and parking lots. Sand is a necessary ingredient in making concrete.

Legend:

Cattle		Maple syrup	
Coal		Mineral mining	
Dairy		Natural gas	
Fruit		Oats	
Grains		Oil	
Grapes		Potatoes	
Hay		Poultry	
Hogs		Sheep	
Manufacturing		Vegetables	

Urban or industrial area
Forests, some farming
Farming

A surgeon reviews the operating room schedule for the Hospital of the University of Pennsylvania.

SEE IT HERE!

DRAKE WELL MUSEUM

Visit the birthplace of the oil industry—the Drake Well Museum. The museum tells the tale of a bold, new industry that changed the United States. See videos and exhibits about oil drilling, as well as an operating oil field and birds! Yes, birds! The area has bald eagles and red-tailed hawks that squabble over which will dominate the skies above the museum.

SERVICES

As in many states, the service industry now contributes more to the economy and employs more people than either manufacturing or agriculture. Services support both the community at large and individuals. Education, health care, and social services make up the largest component of the service industry. People who are employed in these areas include teachers and other school administrators and employees as well as doctors, nurses, and other medical personnel. Social services include those provided by lawyers, social workers, and clergy.

Finance, insurance, and real estate make up one of the next-largest service groups. People in these industries work in banks, provide insurance, and help people sell or buy houses. Financial advisers manage and recommend investments such as stocks and bonds. Many of these financial products are bought and sold on the Philadelphia Stock Exchange.

Tourism is a fast-growing industry in Pennsylvania. Tourism provides jobs in hotels, motels, restaurants, amusement parks, and museums. This industry adds more jobs in transportation, garbage removal, food deliveries, and laundry services. Visitors to the state spend more than $21.5 billion yearly. The industry generates 563,400 jobs and more than $4 billion in annual taxes.

The Philadelphia Stock Exchange is the oldest stock exchange in the United States. It opened for business in 1790 and is still operating.

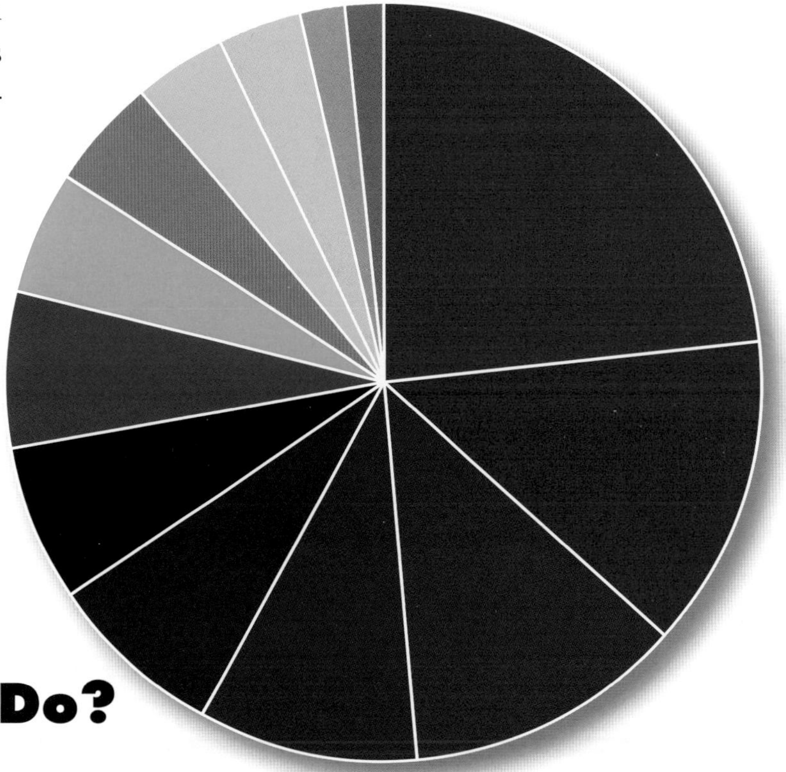

What Do Pennsylvanians Do?

This color-coded chart shows what industries Pennsylvanians work in.

23.6% Educational services, health care, and social assistance, 1,385,015

13.4% Manufacturing, 788,913

11.8% Retail trade, 696,162

9.4% Professional, scientific, management, administrative, and waste management services, 555,547

7.6% Arts, entertainment, recreation, accommodation, and food services, 444,112

6.8% Finance, insurance, real estate, rental, and leasing, 398,198

6.5% Construction, 382,725

5.4% Transportation, warehousing, and utilities, 315,426

4.6% Other services, except public administration, 269,174

4.1% Public administration, 240,239

3.4% Wholesale trade, 199,224

2.2% Information, 126,760

1.4% Agriculture, forestry, fishing, hunting, and mining, 79,620

Source: U.S. Census Bureau, 2006 estimate

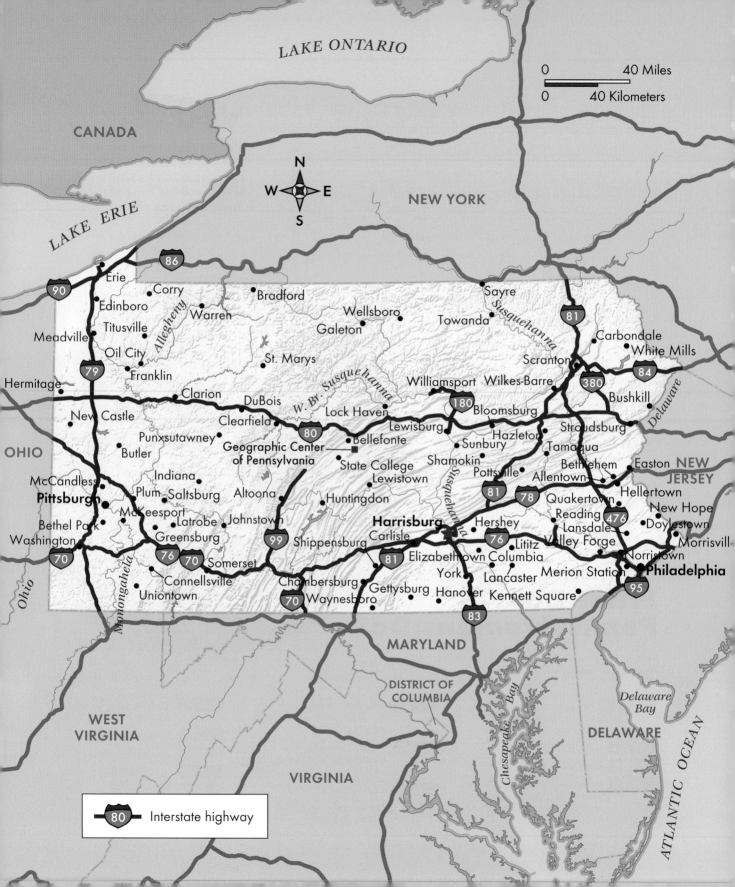

LAKE ONTARIO

CANADA

LAKE ERIE

NEW YORK

| 0 | 40 Miles |
| 0 | 40 Kilometers |

N
W · E
S

86

Erie
Corry
Bradford
Sayre
Edinboro
Warren
Wellsboro
Towanda
90
Titusville
Galeton
Carbondale
Meadville
White Mills
Oil City
St. Marys
Scranton
Wilkes-Barre
Bushkill
84
Hermitage
Franklin
79
81
Clarion
Williamsport
380
New Castle
DuBois
Lock Haven
Bloomsburg
Stroudsburg
Clearfield
Lewisburg
Hazleton
Tamaqua
Punxsutawney
80
Bellefonte
Sunbury
Bethlehem
Easton **NEW**
Butler
Geographic Center
of Pennsylvania
State College
Shamokin
Pottsville
Allentown **JERSEY**
Indiana
Lewistown
81
78
Hellertown
Plum Saltsburg
Altoona
Huntingdon
Quakertown
New Hope
Pittsburgh
Johnstown
Hershey
Reading
Lansdale
476
Doylestown
McKeesport
Latrobe
Harrisburg
76
Valley Forge
Morrisvill
Bethel Park
Greensburg
99
Shippensburg
Carlisle
Lititz
Norristown
Washington
70
76 **70**
Somerset
Elizabethtown
Columbia
Merion Station
Philadelphia
70
Connellsville
Chambersburg
York
Lancaster
95
Uniontown
Waynesboro
Gettysburg
Hanover
Kennett Square

McCandless

OHIO

83

MARYLAND

DISTRICT OF
COLUMBIA

Delaware
Bay

WEST
VIRGINIA

DELAWARE

VIRGINIA

Allegheny
Susquehanna
W. Br. Susquehanna
Monongahela
Ohio
Susquehanna
Delaware
Chesapeake Bay

ATLANTIC OCEAN

80 — Interstate highway

CHAPTER NINE

TRAVEL GUIDE

★

Pennsylvania offers a unique combination of historic areas and natural beauty. What will you find there? Steep mountains and Civil War battlefields, rushing rivers and the Liberty Bell, deep forests and cobblestone streets. In Pennsylvania, you can hike in the Delaware Water Gap or through an art museum. Take a tour and see for yourself.

← Follow along with this travel map. We'll start in Philadelphia and make our way to Pittsburgh.

PHILADELPHIA AND ITS NEIGHBORS

THINGS TO DO: Watch demonstrations of traditional skills, see the Liberty Bell, or step back in time at Valley Forge.

Philadelphia

★ **Independence National Historical Park:** Start your day at one of several historic colonial homes. Visit Independence Hall, then check out the Liberty Bell at Liberty Bell Center. Head to the National Museum of American Jewish History, and stop by the Free Quaker Meeting House. After a long day, take a rest in Franklin Square.

★ **The U.S. Mint:** To visit the mint, you'll need to have a tour arranged by your congressional representative. The Mint displays **commemorative** coins, national medals, and a set of glass mosaics. You'll also see coins being minted. Sorry, no free samples!

Bald eagle silver dollar

WORD TO KNOW

commemorative *intended to honor or remember a person or event*

Independence Hall

★ **Elfreth's Alley:** This colonial street is believed to be the oldest continuously occupied neighborhood in the United States.

★ **Philadelphia Academy of Fine Arts:** Here you can enjoy the works of Mary Cassatt, Georgia O'Keeffe, Benjamin West, and other American artists.

★ **Franklin Institute Science Museum:** You can walk through a supersized model of a human heart or discover the shocking nature of static electricity on your trip through this hands-on science center.

★ **Academy of Natural Sciences:** See the most delicate of species (butterflies) and the most fearsome (dinosaurs) among the many hands-on and crawl-through exhibits at this family-friendly museum.

Red kangaroo

★ **Philadelphia Zoo:** Slither through the reptile house or chatter with the chimps at the new primate facility. The zoo has some rare species: bicolored tamarins, bamboo lemurs, red kangaroos, and Madagascar giant jumping rats.

Merion Station

★ **The Barnes Foundation:** This museum boasts one of the world's finest collections of impressionist art. It includes works by Pierre-Auguste Renoir, Paul Cézanne, Vincent van Gogh, Pablo Picasso, Georges Seurat, and others.

Columbia

★ **National Watch and Clock Museum:** At this museum, you can hear clocks that chime, cuckoo, click, and clack.

★ **Landis Valley Museum:** Thousands of artifacts bring to life the 18th and 19th centuries. On the farm, artisans demonstrate traditional skills such as sheepshearing, candle making, and tinsmithing. There is a tannery, print shop, blacksmith shop, school, firehouse, and country store.

★ **Hopewell Furnace:** The iron produced here was used to make cannonballs and shot for soldiers in the Continental army.

Julius Sturgis Pretzel Bakery

Lititz

★ **Julius Sturgis Pretzel Bakery:** Here's a tour with a delightful twist. See hard and soft pretzels being baked. Enjoy a sample!

★ **Wilbur Chocolate Candy Americana Museum Store:** Follow your nose! That's the sweet scent of handmade chocolate.

Morrisville

★ **Pennsbury Manor:** William Penn's well-preserved home includes several outbuildings (smokehouse, workers' cottage, bake house) as well as farm animals and a kitchen garden.

MILTON S. HERSHEY: A CHOCOHOLIC'S HERO

Milton S. Hershey (1857–1945) was a failure—at first. His first business, making taffy and caramels, failed. Next, he manufactured Hershey's fine candies—and that failed. Finally, he became partners with Harry Lebkicher in the Lancaster Caramel Company and achieved success. Using money earned from the caramels, Hershey started making chocolates, eventually producing 114 different kinds. In 1900, he sold the caramel portion of his business to concentrate on chocolates and introduced the Hershey's Bar.

? Want to know more? See www.dol.gov/oasam/programs/laborhall/2003_hershey.htm

Hershey

★ **Hershey Chocolate World:** See how Hershey's chocolates are made. Nearby, Hershey Park has dozens of rides. When you need a rest, smell the roses and watch the butterflies in Hershey Gardens.

Doylestown

★ **Moravian Pottery and Tile Works:** See what Moravian craftspeople can do with clay.

New Hope

★ **Bowman's Hill Wildflower Preserve:** At this site, you can follow trails that wind through flower-dotted meadows, woods, and wetlands. Watch birds flock to the feeders as you rest at the observation station.

Valley Forge

★ **Valley Forge National Historical Park:** On a visit to this park, learn about the hardships endured by General George Washington's army in the historic winter of 1777.

Visitors to Washington's headquarters at Valley Forge National Historical Park

Longwood Gardens

Kennett Square

★ **Longwood Gardens:** Stunning gardens with rare and unusual trees and lush flower beds. The more than 11,000 plant species include **topiaries**, fountains, and a children's garden.

WORD TO KNOW

topiaries *plants or trees trimmed into fantastic shapes*

Easton

★ **National Canal Museum:** Learn about the people who worked on canals, the animals that pulled the boats, and how canals were built. Outside, take a ride on a restored section of the Lackawanna Canal.

★ **Crayola Factory:** See how Crayola crayons are made and then do your own coloring. Make a book, birthday card, poster, or name tag.

Each year, Crayola produces 2 billion crayons in 120 colors and labeled in 120 different languages. Crayola crayons are used in 80 countries throughout the world.

THE POCONOS

THINGS TO DO: Take a ride into a mine, browse through museums, or explore a fossil trail.

Bloomsburg

★ **Covered Bridge Tour:** A route from Bloomsburg to Elysburg crosses six covered bridges. The tour ends at Knoebels Amusement Resort, an old-fashioned, carnival-style park.

Scranton

★ **Lackawanna Coal Mine:** Want to experience what a coal miner does for a living? Climb into a yellow transport car that takes you 300 feet (90 m) down into the mine. A former miner escorts you on a fascinating walking tour, where you'll hear all about the underground life of a miner.

Delaware Water Gap National Recreation Area

Bushkill

★ **Delaware Water Gap National Recreation Area:** There's lots to do at the Delaware Water Gap. Hike up Mount Tammany, listen to the cascading waterfalls, or explore a fossil trail.

White Mills

★ **Dorflinger Glass Museum:** This small museum has a long history—it produced crystal for President Lincoln. Today, it offers exquisite examples of cut and etched glass.

Allentown

★ **Museum of Indian Culture:** Long ago, people made what they needed by using skills that were passed down from generation to generation. Here, you'll have a chance to try your hand at making rope from plant fibers or lighting a fire. You can also enjoy traditional Native American music and dance.

Hellertown

★ **Lost River Caverns:** Here you can see five lofty chambers of crystal formations, dazzling gems, **stalactites**, **stalagmites**, and rocks that glow in the dark.

WORDS TO KNOW

stalactites *columns or pillars formed on the roof of a cave from dripping groundwater*

stalagmites *columns or pillars formed on the floor of a cave from dripping groundwater*

CENTRAL PENNSYLVANIA

THINGS TO DO: Hike the trails around the Grand Canyon of Pennsylvania, learn about the history of Little League baseball, or honor the sacrifices of Civil War soldiers at Gettysburg National Military Park.

Galeton

★ **Pennsylvania Lumber Museum:** How did "woodhicks" (lumbermen) live? What was their workday like? You'll find out here as you walk through a coal-powered logging train and peer into a bunkhouse at this reproduction lumber camp.

Wellsboro

★ **Grand Canyon of Pennsylvania:**
The sharp cliff sides are heavily
forested along this 50-mile-long
(80 km) stretch of Pine Creek.
Trails lead from the cliff tops to the
refreshing creek at the bottom.

State College

★ **Palmer Museum of Art:** This
museum displays work spanning
35 centuries of creativity.

Williamsport

★ **Little League Baseball Museum:**
Here you can find out how Little
League baseball got its start, work
out in the batting cage, or visit
the Hall of Excellence, which has
stories about Little Leaguers who
grew up to become successful in
other fields.

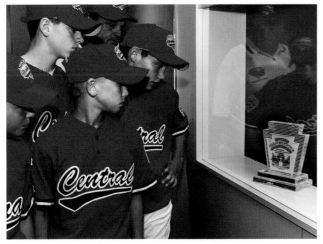

Visitors at the Little League Baseball Museum

Students touring the Gettysburg National Military Park

Gettysburg

★ **Gettysburg National Military
Park:** Tour the historic battle-
field and cemetery that inspired
Abraham Lincoln's Gettysburg
Address.

★ **Civil War Historic Trails:** No
area in the North saw as much
military activity during the Civil
War as the Cumberland Valley.
From York to Wrightsville,
Hanover to Harrisburg, Carlisle
to Chambersburg, and ending at
Gettysburg, road markers and
period buildings commemorate
this tragic and pivotal time in
American history.

IN THE WEST

THINGS TO DO: Watch the birds at Presque Isle or shop the Strip in Pittsburgh.

Erie

★ **Presque Isle State Park:** Go fly a kite! Or sail, water-ski, and laze on the beach. Bird-watchers flock to the site to see the many birds that stop by on their spring and fall migrations. Blue herons strut through the reeds, and sandpipers skitter along the shoreline.

The lighthouse at Presque Isle State Park

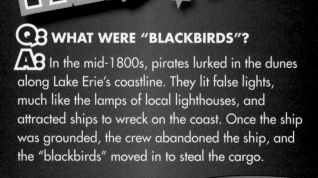

FAQ ★ ★ ★

Q: WHAT WERE "BLACKBIRDS"?

A: In the mid-1800s, pirates lurked in the dunes along Lake Erie's coastline. They lit false lights, much like the lamps of local lighthouses, and attracted ships to wreck on the coast. Once the ship was grounded, the crew abandoned the ship, and the "blackbirds" moved in to steal the cargo.

★ **Brucker Great Blue Heron Sanctuary:** In spring and summer, more than 250 breeding pairs of great blue herons nest in the preserve, and viewers can watch the herons build their nests, sit on eggs, and feed their nestlings.

The Alleghenies

★ **Allegheny National Forest:** This land is rugged, wild, and, in places, ancient. Remnants of old-growth forest remain.

Titusville

★ **Drake Well Museum:** This is where the oil industry started and is a great place to learn how oil changed history.

Saltsburg

★ **Thunder Mountain:** Each August, the Thunder Mountain Lenape hold a festival and powwow that features storytelling, crafts, and traditional music and dance, as well as hands-on events for children.

Pittsburgh

★ **Strip District:** At this indoor-outdoor market, shoppers buy from greengrocers, fishmongers, butchers, and florists. They can also snack on barbecue-on-a-stick, cannoli, grilled sausage, or other treats. Street vendors set up stalls with clothing, CDs, crafts, and leather goods.

★ **The Andy Warhol Museum:** Andy Warhol is honored at the museum that bears his name. Exhibits of his prints and paintings change constantly and are often based on themes, such as famous people or familiar everyday items.

In 2007, Andy Warhol's painting of a car crash, *Green Burning Car I,* sold for $71.1 million at an auction in New York City.

★ **John H. Heinz Pittsburgh Regional History Center:** Climb aboard a trolley that once ran through Pittsburgh, learn what it was like to live in a log cabin 200 years ago, or be a steelworker 100 years ago. You'll also find out about the people from many parts of the world who made Pittsburgh their home.

★ **National Aviary:** More than 400 species of birds—some threatened or endangered in the wild—live in habitats that mimic nature. Many of the birds fly freely in this **aviary**.

WORD TO KNOW

aviary *a large walk-in enclosure where birds have room to fly*

Phipps Conservatory

★ **Phipps Conservatory:** Sit in one of the largest glass buildings in the nation and take in the beauty of hundreds of plant species. The Discovery Garden is a hands-on children's exhibit.

★ **Carnegie Museum of Natural History:** If it is animal, vegetable, or mineral, this museum has a sample on display. There are halls for dinosaurs, birds, minerals, and major habitats.

★ **Carnegie Science Center:** Science rocks! And rolls! Here you can learn about science through games such as "Make Your Own Earthquake" and "Spin Up a Hurricane." SeaScape offers a Pacific coral reef and a touch tank with living, touchable critters. A planetarium and an Omnimax theater round out your time here.

WRITING PROJECTS

Check out these ideas for creating a campaign brochure and writing you-are-there narratives. Or research the lives of famous people from the state.

ART PROJECTS

You can illustrate the state song, create a dazzling PowerPoint presentation, or learn about the state quarter and design your own.

TIMELINE

What happened when? This timeline highlights important events in the state's history—and shows what was happening throughout the United States at the same time.

FAST FACTS

Use this section to find fascinating facts about state symbols, land area and population statistics, weather, sports teams, and much more.

GLOSSARY

Remember the Words to Know from the chapters in this book? They're all collected here.

SCIENCE, TECHNOLOGY, & MATH PROJECTS

Make weather maps, graph population statistics, and research endangered species that live in the state.

120

PRIMARY VS. SECONDARY SOURCES

121

So what are primary and secondary sources? And what's the diff? This section explains all that and where you can find them.

BIOGRAPHICAL DICTIONARY

133

This at-a-glance guide highlights some of the state's most important and influential people. Visit this section and read about their contributions to the state, the country, and the world.

RESOURCES

Books, Web sites, DVDs, and more. Take a look at these additional sources for information about the state.

137

WRITING PROJECTS

★ ★ ★

Write a Memoir, Journal, or Editorial for Your School Newspaper!

Picture Yourself . . .

★ Building a Lenni Lenape longhouse. What supplies would you need and where would you find them? Describe how you would build it. Who would live in the longhouse?

SEE: Chapter Two, page 30.
GO TO: www.lenapelifeways.org/lenape2.htm

★ Working in a Pennsylvania coal mine. What is it like down in the mines? Describe the sounds, sights, and smells. Also describe the housing where you live.

SEE: Chapter Four, pages 52, 56–57.
GO TO: www.phmc.state.pa.us/ppet/miningmuseum/page1.asp?secid=31

Create an Election Brochure or Web Site!

Run for office! Throughout this book, you've read about some of the issues that concern Pennsylvania today. As a candidate for governor of Pennsylvania, create a campaign brochure or Web site.

★ Explain how you meet the qualifications to be governor of Pennsylvania.

★ Talk about the three or four major issues you'll focus on if you're elected.

★ Remember, you'll be responsible for Pennsylvania's budget. How would you spend the taxpayers' money?

SEE: Chapter Seven, page 90.

GO TO: Pennsylvania's government Web site at www.state.pa.us. You might also want to read some local newspapers. Try these:

Philadelphia Inquirer at www.philly.com/inquirer

Pittsburgh Post-Gazette at www.post-gazette.com

Create an interview script with a famous person from Pennsylvania!

★ Research various Pennsylvanians, such as Rachel Carson, William Penn, Benjamin Franklin, Andrew Carnegie, Gifford Pinchot, Marian Anderson, Jim Thorpe, Christina Aguilera, Kate DiCamillo, or Will Smith.

★ Based on your research, pick one person you would most like to talk with.

★ Write a script of the interview. What questions would you ask? How would this person answer? Create a question-and-answer format. You may want to supplement this writing project with a voice-recording dramatization of the interview.

SEE: Chapters One, Three, Four, Five, and Six, pages 22, 36, 50, 52, 63, 82, 85 and the Biographical Dictionary, pages 133–136.

GO TO: The Pennsylvania Hall of Fame at www.geocities.com/Heartland/4547/pindex.html

ART PROJECTS

★ ★ ★

Create a PowerPoint Presentation or Visitors' Guide

Welcome to Pennsylvania!

Pennsylvania is a great place to visit and to live! From its natural beauty to its bustling cities and historical sites, there's plenty to see and do. In your PowerPoint presentation or brochure, highlight 10 to 15 of Pennsylvania's amazing landmarks. Be sure to include:

★ a map of the state showing where these sites are located

★ photos, illustrations, Web links, natural history facts, geographic stats, climate and weather, plants and wildlife, and recent discoveries

SEE: Chapter Nine, pages 106–115, and Fast Facts, pages 126–127.

GO TO: The official tourism Web site for Pennsylvania at www.visitpa.com. Download and print maps, photos, and vacation ideas for tourists.

Illustrate the Lyrics to the Pennsylvania State Song

("Pennsylvania")

Use markers, paints, photos, collages, colored pencils, or computer graphics to illustrate the lyrics to "Pennsylvania." Turn your illustrations into a picture book, or scan them into PowerPoint and add music.

SEE: The lyrics to "Pennsylvania" on page 128.

GO TO: The Pennsylvania state government Web site at www.state.pa.us to find out more about the origin of the state song.

State Quarter Project

From 1999 to 2008, the U.S. Mint introduced new quarters commemorating each of the 50 states in the order that they were admitted to the Union. Each state's quarter features a unique design on its back, or reverse.

GO TO: www.usmint.gov/kids and find out what's featured on the back of the Pennsylvania quarter.

★ Research the significance of the image. Who designed the quarter? Who chose the final design?

★ Design your own Pennsylvania quarter. What images would you choose for the reverse?

★ Make a poster showing the Pennsylvania quarter and label each image.

SCIENCE, TECHNOLOGY, & MATH PROJECTS

★ ★ ★

Graph Population Statistics!

★ Compare population statistics (such as ethnic background, birth, death, and literacy rates) in Pennsylvania counties or major cities.

★ In your graph or chart, look at population density and write sentences describing what the population statistics show; graph one set of population statistics and write a paragraph explaining what the graphs reveal.

SEE: Chapter Six, pages 72–76.

GO TO: The official Web site for the U.S. Census Bureau at www.census.gov and at http://quickfacts.census.gov/qfd/states/42000.html to find out more about population statistics, how they work, and what the statistics are for Pennsylvania.

Create a Weather Map of Pennsylvania!

Use your knowledge of Pennsylvania's geography to research and identify conditions that result in specific weather events. What is it about the geography of Pennsylvania that makes it vulnerable to flooding? Create a weather map or poster that shows the weather patterns over the state. Include a caption explaining the technology used to measure weather phenomena and provide data.

SEE: Chapter One, pages 16–18.

GO TO: The National Oceanic and Atmospheric Administration's National Weather Service Web site at www.weather.gov for weather maps and forecasts for Pennsylvania.

Track Endangered Species

Using your knowledge of Pennsylvania's wildlife, research which animals and plants are endangered or threatened.

★ Find out what the state is doing to protect these species.

★ Chart known populations of the animals and plants, and report on changes in certain geographic areas.

SEE: Chapter One, page 20.

GO TO: Web sites such as http://ecos.fws.gov/tess_public/StateListingAndOccurrence.do?state=PA for lists of endangered species in Pennsylvania.

Mud salamander

PRIMARY VS. SECONDARY SOURCES

★　★　★

What's the Diff?

Your teacher may require at least one or two primary sources and one or two secondary sources for your assignment. So, what's the difference between the two?

★ **Primary sources are original.** You are reading the actual words of someone's diary, journal, letter, autobiography, or interview. Primary sources can also be photographs, maps, prints, cartoons, news/film footage, posters, first-person newspaper articles, drawings, musical scores, and recordings. By the way, when you conduct a survey, interview someone, shoot a video, or take photographs to include in a project, you are creating primary sources!

★ **Secondary sources are what you find in encyclopedias, textbooks, articles, biographies, and almanacs.** These are written by a person or group of people who tell about something that happened to someone else. Secondary sources also recount what another person said or did. This book is an example of a secondary source.

Now that you know what primary sources are—where can you find them?

★ **Your school or local library:** Check the library catalog for collections of original writings, government documents, musical scores, and so on. Some of this material may be stored on microfilm. The Library of Congress Web site (www.loc.gov) is an excellent online resource for primary source materials.

★ **Historical societies:** These organizations keep historical documents, photographs, and other materials. Staff members can help you find what you are looking for. History museums are also great places to see primary sources firsthand.

★ **The Internet:** There are lots of sites that have primary sources you can download and use in a project or assignment.

TIMELINE

★ ★ ★

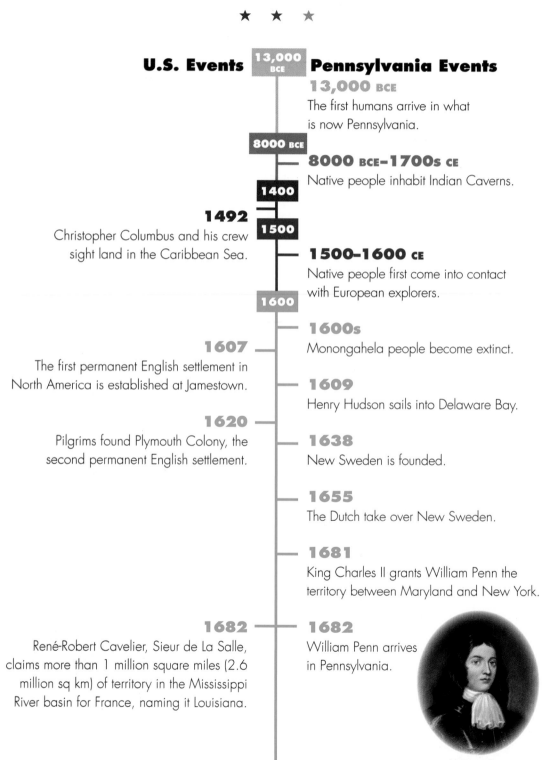

U.S. Events | 13,000 BCE | **Pennsylvania Events**

13,000 BCE
The first humans arrive in what is now Pennsylvania.

8000 BCE

8000 BCE–1700s CE
Native people inhabit Indian Caverns.

1400

1492
Christopher Columbus and his crew sight land in the Caribbean Sea.

1500

1500–1600 CE
Native people first come into contact with European explorers.

1600

1600s
Monongahela people become extinct.

1607
The first permanent English settlement in North America is established at Jamestown.

1609
Henry Hudson sails into Delaware Bay.

1620
Pilgrims found Plymouth Colony, the second permanent English settlement.

1638
New Sweden is founded.

1655
The Dutch take over New Sweden.

1681
King Charles II grants William Penn the territory between Maryland and New York.

1682
René-Robert Cavelier, Sieur de La Salle, claims more than 1 million square miles (2.6 million sq km) of territory in the Mississippi River basin for France, naming it Louisiana.

1682
William Penn arrives in Pennsylvania.

William Penn

U.S. Events `1700` Pennsylvania Events

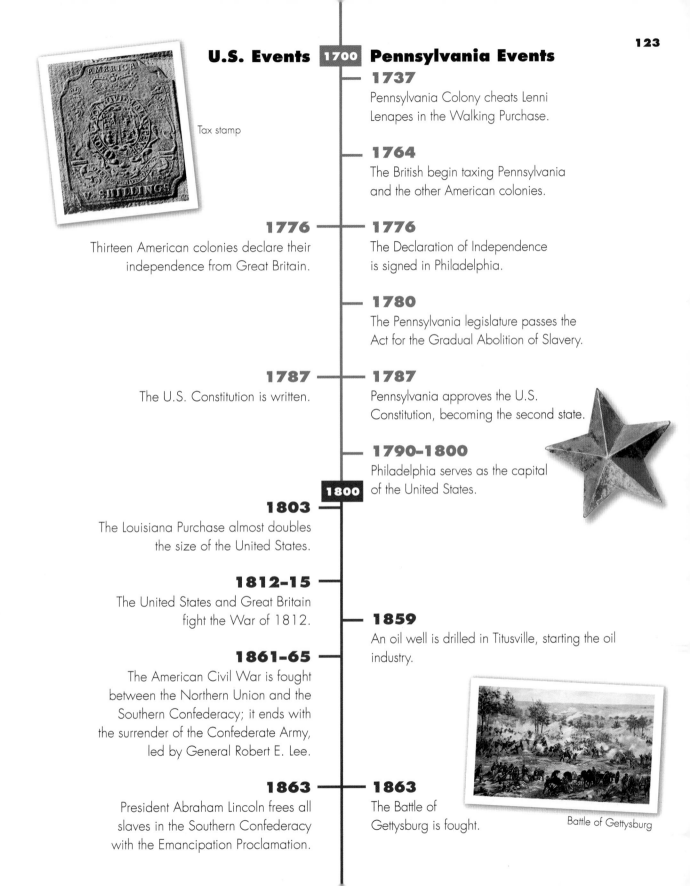

Tax stamp

1737
Pennsylvania Colony cheats Lenni Lenapes in the Walking Purchase.

1764
The British begin taxing Pennsylvania and the other American colonies.

1776
Thirteen American colonies declare their independence from Great Britain.

1776
The Declaration of Independence is signed in Philadelphia.

1780
The Pennsylvania legislature passes the Act for the Gradual Abolition of Slavery.

1787
The U.S. Constitution is written.

1787
Pennsylvania approves the U.S. Constitution, becoming the second state.

1790–1800
Philadelphia serves as the capital of the United States.

`1800`

1803
The Louisiana Purchase almost doubles the size of the United States.

1812–15
The United States and Great Britain fight the War of 1812.

1859
An oil well is drilled in Titusville, starting the oil industry.

1861–65
The American Civil War is fought between the Northern Union and the Southern Confederacy; it ends with the surrender of the Confederate Army, led by General Robert E. Lee.

1863
President Abraham Lincoln frees all slaves in the Southern Confederacy with the Emancipation Proclamation.

1863
The Battle of Gettysburg is fought.

Battle of Gettysburg

U.S. Events

Pennsylvania Events

1889
More than 2,200 people die in the Johnstown flood.

1898
The United States gains control of Cuba, Puerto Rico, the Philippines, and Guam after defeating Spain in the Spanish-American War.

1900

1915
African Americans from the South begin moving north in the Great Migration.

1917-18
The United States engages in World War I.

1920
The Nineteenth Amendment to the U.S. Constitution grants women the right to vote.

1920
The first commercial broadcast radio station is introduced in Pittsburgh.

1929
The stock market crashes, plunging the United States more deeply into the Great Depression.

1941-45
The United States engages in World War II.

1941-45
Pennsylvania supplies about one-third of America's steel during World War II.

1951-53
The United States engages in the Korean War.

1958
Robert Nix is elected Pennsylvania's first African American congressman.

1964-73
The United States engages in the Vietnam War.

1979
The incident at Three Mile Island makes Americans rethink nuclear energy.

1991
The United States and other nations engage in the brief Persian Gulf War against Iraq.

2000

2001
Terrorists hijack four U.S. aircraft and crash them into the World Trade Center in New York City, the Pentagon in Arlington, Virginia, and a Pennsylvania field, killing thousands.

2001
On September 11, United Flight 93 crashes near Shanksville, after passengers try to wrest control of the plane from hijackers. It is believed the hijackers intended to crash the plane into the White House or U.S. Capitol.

2003
The United States and coalition forces invade Iraq.

2006
WiFi Downtown Pittsburgh begins, allowing citizens to connect to the Internet anywhere downtown.

Wi-Fi HOTSPOT

GLOSSARY

★ ★ ★

amendment a change to a law or legal document

aviary a large walk-in enclosure where birds have room to fly

boycott the organized refusal to use a service or buy a product, as a form of protest

carcinogen something that causes cancer

charter a document from a ruler granting rights to a group

commemorative intended to honor or remember a person or event

confederation an association of groups that come together with common goals

conservation the act of saving or preserving something, such as a natural resource, plant, or animal species

erosion the gradual wearing away of rock or soil by physical breakdown, chemical solution, or water

industrialists business owners who are engaged in the manufacture of goods

integrate to end segregation and provide everyone equal access or membership

pesticides any chemicals or biological agents used to kill plant or animal pests

petrochemicals chemicals produced from oil or natural gas

plateau an elevated part of the earth with steep slopes

precipitation all water that falls to the earth, including rain, sleet, hail, snow, dew, fog, or mist

radiation energy that is given off in the form of waves or particles

rationed controlled the amount one could use

reactor a device for the controlled release of nuclear energy

revenue the money a government receives through taxes and other sources

stalactites columns or pillars formed on the roof of a cave from dripping groundwater

stalagmites columns or pillars formed on the floor of a cave from dripping groundwater

stock a share in the ownership of a company

strikes organized refusals to work, usually as a sign of protest about working conditions

suffrage the right to vote

synthetic related to something that doesn't occur in nature

topiaries plants or trees trimmed into fantastic shapes

FAST FACTS

★ ★ ★

State Symbols

Statehood date	December 12, 1787, the 2nd state
Origin of state name	William Penn suggested that the colony be called Sylvania, which means "wooded." King Charles II added "Penn" to "Sylvania" in honor of Penn's father.
State capital	Harrisburg
State nickname	Keystone State
State motto	Virtue, liberty and independence
State bird	Ruffed grouse
State flower	Mountain laurel
State fish	Brook trout
State song	"Pennsylvania" (See lyrics on page 128)
State tree	Hemlock
State fair	Harrisburg, second week in June

State seal

Geography

Total area; rank	46,055 square miles (119,282 sq km); 33rd
Land; rank	44,817 square miles (116,076 sq km); 32nd
Water; rank	1,239 square miles (3,209 sq km); 28th
Inland water; rank	490 square miles (1,269 sq km); 33rd
Great Lakes water; rank	749 square miles (1,940 sq km); 7th
Geographic center	2.5 miles (4 km) southwest of Bellefonte
Latitude	39°43' N and 42° N
Longitude	74°43' W and 80°31' W
Highest point	Mount Davis, 3,213 feet (979 m) above sea level in Somerset County
Lowest point	Sea level at the Delaware River
Largest city	Philadelphia
Number of counties	67
Longest river	Susquehanna

Population

Population; rank (2007 estimate)	12,432,792; 6th
Density (2007 estimate)	277 persons per square mile (107 per sq km)
Population distribution (2000 census)	77% urban, 23% rural
Race (2007 estimate)	White persons: 85.6%*
	Black persons: 10.8%*
	Asian persons: 2.4%*
	American Indian and Alaska Native persons: 0.2%*
	Native Hawaiian and Other Pacific Islanders: 0.1%*
	Persons reporting two or more races: 1.0%
	Persons of Hispanic or Latino origin: 4.5%†
	White persons not Hispanic: 81.8%

Includes persons reporting only one race.
† Hispanics may be of any race, so they are also included in applicable race categories.

Weather

Record high temperature	111°F (44°C) at Phoenixville on July 10, 1936
Record low temperature	−42°F (−41°C) at Smethport on January 5, 1904
Average July temperature	78°F (26°C)
Average January temperature	32°F (0°C)
Average yearly precipitation	42 inches (107 cm)

State flag

STATE SONG

★ ★ ★

"Pennsylvania"

Eddie Khoury wrote the words to the Pennsylvania state song, and Ronnie Bonner wrote the music. The song was officially adopted in 1990.

Pennsylvania, Pennsylvania,
Mighty is your name,
Steeped in glory and tradition,
Object of acclaim.
Where brave men fought the foe of freedom,
Tyranny decried,
'Till the bell of independence
filled the countryside.

Chorus:
Pennsylvania, Pennsylvania,
May your future be,
filled with honor everlasting
as your history.

Pennsylvania, Pennsylvania,
Blessed by God's own hand,
Birthplace of a mighty nation,
Keystone of the land.
Where first our country's flag unfolded,
Freedom to proclaim,
May the voices of tomorrow
glorify your name.
(Chorus)

NATURAL AREAS AND HISTORIC SITES

★ ★ ★

National Recreation Area

The *Delaware Water Gap National Recreation Area* includes 40 miles (64 km) of the Middle Delaware River that cuts through the low-forested mountain ridge.

National Scenic & Recreational River

Upper Delaware Scenic & Recreational River hugs the boundary between Pennsylvania and New York and is the longest free-flowing river in the northeastern United States.

National Memorials

The *Johnstown Flood National Memorial* commemorates the site where more than 2,200 people died when the South Fork Dam broke on May 31, 1889.

The *Flight 93 National Memorial* honors the heroes aboard United Airlines Flight 93, who thwarted a planned air attack on Washington, D.C., on September 11, 2001.

National Battlefield

Fort Necessity National Battlefield commemorates a battle site from the French and Indian War.

National Military Park

Gettysburg National Military Park preserves the grounds of the Civil War battle, as well as *Gettysburg National Cemetery*, where President Lincoln delivered the Gettysburg Address.

National Scenic Trails

Three national scenic trails pass through Pennsylvania: the *Appalachian National Scenic Trail*, the *North Country National Scenic Trail*, and the *Potomac Heritage National Scenic Trail*.

National Historical Parks

Independence National Historical Park, in Philadelphia, is the home of the Liberty Bell and Independence Hall, where the U.S. Constitution and Declaration of Independence were signed.

Valley Forge National Historical Park honors the struggle of George Washington and his troops in the winter of 1777.

National Historic Sites

Pennsylvania is home to seven national historic sites: *Allegheny Portage Railroad National Historic Site*, *Edgar Allan Poe National Historic Site*, *Eisenhower National Historic Site*, *Friendship Hill National Historic Site*, *Gloria Dei Church National Historic Site*, *Hopewell Furnace National Historic Site*, and the *Steamtown National Historic Site*.

State Parks and Forests

Pennsylvania's state park system maintains 120 state parks and recreational areas. The state also has 19 state forests.

SPORTS TEAMS

★　★　★

NCAA Teams (Division I)

Bucknell University *Bison*
Drexel University *Dragons*
Duquesne University *Dukes*
Lafayette College *Leopards*
La Salle University *Explorers*
Lehigh University *Mountain Hawks*
Pennsylvania State University *Nittany Lions*

Robert Morris College *Colonials*
St. Francis College *Red Flash*
St. Joseph's University *Hawks*
Temple University *Owls*
University of Pennsylvania *Quakers*
University of Pittsburgh *Panthers*
Villanova University *Wildcats*

PROFESSIONAL SPORTS TEAMS

★　★　★

Major League Baseball

Philadelphia *Phillies*
Pittsburgh *Pirates*

National Football League

Philadelphia *Eagles*
Pittsburgh *Steelers*

National Basketball Association

Philadelphia *76ers*

National Hockey League

Philadelphia *Flyers*
Pittsburgh *Penguins*

CULTURAL INSTITUTIONS

Libraries

The *Carnegie Library of Pittsburgh* was donated to the city in 1895 by philanthropist Andrew Carnegie. It has 18 branches throughout Pittsburgh and has large children's, science, and art collections.

The *David Library of the American Revolution* in Washington Crossing has materials from 1750 to 1800, including the Revolutionary War. It is built on a farm and holds more than 40,000 items in print and 10,000 documents on microfilm.

The *Historical Society of Pennsylvania Library*, in Philadelphia, is one of the oldest historical societies in the United States. It has more than 500,000 books, 300,000 graphic materials, and 1.5 million manuscripts.

The *State Library of Pennsylvania* traces itself back to 1745 and Benjamin Franklin, who created it as a research library for statesmen. Today, it serves not only legislators but also the general public.

Museums

Carnegie Science Center (Pittsburgh) includes an Omnimax theater, a World War II submarine, a planetarium, and hundreds of science exhibits.

Carnegie Museum of Natural History (Pittsburgh) holds 21 million objects and specimens, of which 15,000 are on display.

Franklin Institute Science Museum (Philadelphia) features numerous exhibits on history and science. It also has a planetarium.

The *National Civil War Museum* (Harrisburg) is the only museum in the United States that portrays the entire story of the American Civil War.

Philadelphia Museum of Art houses more than 300,000 works in 200 galleries.

The State Museum of Pennsylvania (Harrisburg) was founded by Benjamin Franklin. It contains more than 3 million objects associated with the history and heritage of Pennsylvania.

Performing Arts

Pennsylvania has five major opera companies, five symphony orchestras, four major dance companies, and two major theater companies.

Universities and Colleges

In 2006, Pennsylvania had 58 public and 173 private institutions of higher learning.

ANNUAL EVENTS

January–March

Mummers Parade in Philadelphia (January 1)

Pennsylvania Farm Show in Harrisburg (second week in January)

Pennsylvania Cross-Country Sled Dog Championship in Marshburg (January)

Groundhog Day Festivities in Punxsutawney (early February)

Charter Day around the state (March)

Maple Sugar Festival in Audubon (March)

Philadelphia Flower Show (March)

Pennsylvania National Arts and Crafts Show in Harrisburg (late March)

April–June

Cherry Blossom Festival of Greater Philadelphia (April)

Bach Music Festival in Bethlehem (May)

Armed Forces Air Show in Avoca (June)

Three Rivers Arts Festival in Pittsburgh (June)

Pennsylvania State Fair in Harrisburg (mid-June)

Civil War Heritage Days in Gettysburg (late June)

July–September

Bark Peelers' Convention near Galeton (early July)

Freedom Festival in Philadelphia (early July)

Pittsburgh Three Rivers Regatta (early July)

Oil Heritage Festival in Oil City (July)

Central Pennsylvania Festival of the Arts in State College (mid-July)

Kunstfest in Ambridge (mid-July)

Shippensburg Corn Festival (August)

Woodsmen's Show near Galeton (August)

Little League Baseball World Series in South Williamsport (late August)

Ligonier Highland Games (early September)

Covered Bridge Festival in Stahlstown (September)

Mushroom Festival in Kennett Square (September)

McClure Bean Soup Festival and Fair (mid-September)

October–December

Apple Harvest Festival in Arendtsville (October)

Covered Bridge and Arts Festival in Elysburg and Forks (October)

Pennsylvania National Horse Show in Harrisburg (late October)

Chrysanthemum Festival in Kennett Square (October–November)

Reenactment of Washington Crossing the Delaware at Washington Crossing Historic Park (December 25)

Mummers Parade

Christina Aguilera (1980–) is a singer and songwriter who grew up in Pittsburgh. Her music ranges from pop to dance to Latin.

Lloyd Alexander (1924–2007) wrote science fiction and fantasy books for children, including *The Black Cauldron, Taran Wanderer,* and *The High King.* He won the Newbery Medal and *School Library Journal's* Best Book of the Year, and was a National Book Award Finalist for Fiction. He was born in Philadelphia.

Marian Anderson See page 82.

Poul Anderson (1926–2001) was a giant in the science-fiction genre. Among his works are *Tau Zero, Twilight World: A Science Fiction Novel of Tomorrow's Children, Brain Wave,* and *The High Crusade.* He was born in Bristol.

Michael Andretti (1962–), who was born in Bethlehem, is a race car driver. He has competed in the Indianapolis 500.

Christina Aguilera

Kobe Bryant

Kevin Bacon (1958–) is an actor who has appeared in films such as *Apollo 13* and *Footloose.* He was born in Philadelphia.

Stan Berenstain (1923–2005) and his wife, **Jan Berenstain (1923–)**, both born in Philadelphia, wrote many delightful children's books about the antics of the Berenstain Bears. The Berenstain Bears have appeared in TV shows and as toys.

Nellie Bly (1864–1922) was a journalist who sometimes went undercover when researching stories. She had herself committed to a hospital for the mentally ill in order to investigate the treatment of patients there. Later, she copied the idea of Jules Verne's novel *Around the World in 80 Days* by making the journey in 72 days, 6 hours, and 11 minutes.

Daniel Boone See page 40.

Kobe Bryant (1978–) is an all-star basketball player for the Los Angeles Lakers. He was born in Philadelphia.

James Buchanan See page 94.

Andrew Carnegie See page 52.

Rachel Carson See page 22.

Mary Cassatt See page 81.

George Catlin (1796–1872), a native of Wilkes-Barre, spent much of his adult life traveling the West and painting the Native Americans there.

Wilt Chamberlain See page 84.

Dick Clark (1929–) is recognizable from his years of hosting TV coverage of New Year's Eve in New York City's Times Square. Clark's TV show *American Bandstand*, which was broadcast from Philadelphia's WFIL, was must-see TV for teens in the 1960s.

Charles "Pete" Conrad (1930–1999) was an astronaut who, in 1969, became one of a handful of people to have walked on the moon. He was from Philadelphia.

Kate DiCamillo

Bill Cosby

Bill Cosby (1937–) is a comedian and actor born in Philadelphia. He broke into television with the show *I Spy*. He also starred in *The Cosby Show*, a sitcom about family life, which aired from 1984 to 1992 and earned several Emmy Awards.

Kate DiCamillo (1964–), who was born in Philadelphia, is a Newbery Medal–winning author of children's novels. Her works include *Because of Winn-Dixie*, *The Tale of Despereaux*, and *The Miraculous Journey of Edward Tulane*.

Walter E. Diemer (1905–1998), a native of Philadelphia, invented bubble gum. He worked for Fleer Corporation, which named his product Dubble Bubble. He taught salesmen how to blow bubbles to boost sales.

Thomas Eakins (1844–1916) was a painter who created realistic and penetrating portraits of the people of Philadelphia. He was also a sculptor and a photographer.

Stephen Foster (1826–1864) of Lawrenceville wrote classic songs such as "Camptown Races," "Oh! Susanna," and "Beautiful Dreamer."

Benjamin Franklin See page 50.

Jim Furyk (1970–) of West Chester is a champion golfer. He won the U.S. Open in 2003.

Stan Getz (1927–1991) was a world-class jazz saxophone player. He was born in Philadelphia.

Ken Griffey Jr. (1969–) has played major league baseball for the Seattle Mariners and the Cincinnati Reds. A center fielder, he has hit more than 600 home runs during his career. He was born in Donora.

Henry J. Heinz See page 102.

Milton S. Hershey See page 110.

Reggie Jackson (1946–), a native of Wyncote, was a baseball star on the New York Yankees in the 1970s. He was named World Series Most Valuable Player in 1973 and 1977, and was inducted into the Baseball Hall of Fame in 1993.

Robert Jackson (1892–1954) served as U.S. attorney general and a justice on the Supreme Court. He also served as U.S. chief counsel at the Nuremberg war crimes trials that prosecuted Germany's Nazi leadership after World War II. He was born in Spring Creek Township.

Arnold Palmer

Suzy Kolber

Suzy Kolber (1964–) is a broadcast journalist best known for her role as a football sideline reporter for ESPN. She was born in Philadelphia.

E. L. Konigsburg (1930–) is a writer who is best known for her book *From the Mixed-up Files of Mrs. Basil E. Frankweiler*. She grew up in Phoenixville and Farrell.

Dan Marino (1961–), a native of Pittsburgh, is a Football Hall of Fame quarterback. He played in eight Super Bowls during his career with the Miami Dolphins but never won.

Arnold Palmer (1929–) is one of the greatest golfers of all time, winning 95 tournaments over his long career. He was born in Latrobe.

Robert Peary (1856–1920) was an explorer who was born in Cresson. He made several expeditions through the Arctic by dogsled.

William Penn See page 36.

Gifford Pinchot See page 63.

Pink (1979–) is a pop, rock, and rhythm-and-blues singer and songwriter who was born Alecia Beth Moore in Doylestown. Her first album, *Can't Take Me Home*, was a major hit. She has won two Grammy Awards for her singing.

Fred Rogers (1928–2003), known to millions of children as Mr. Rogers, was born in Latrobe. He was an educator, Protestant minister, and television host. His show, *Mr. Rogers' Neighborhood*, aired from 1968 to 2001.

Betsy Ross See page 46.

Bayard Rustin See page 66.

M. Night Shyamalan (1970–) is a movie director who was born in India and raised in Penn Valley. His films include *The Sixth Sense* and *The Village*.

Will Smith (1968–) grew up in Philadelphia and became a Grammy Award–winning hip-hop artist under the name Fresh Prince. He later became an actor, starring in the hit TV show *The Fresh Prince of Bel-Air* and in films such as *Men in Black* and *The Pursuit of Happyness*.

M. Night Shyamalan

Thaddeus Stevens See page 56.

William Still See page 51.

Jim Thorpe See page 85.

Honus Wagner (1874–1955), from Pittsburgh, was a baseball player known as the Flying Dutchman. He was one of the first five members of the Baseball Hall of Fame.

Ethel Waters (1896–1977) was an actress and singer who sang jazz, big band, gospel, and popular music. In the 1950s, she starred in her own television show, *Beulah*. She was from Chester.

George Westinghouse (1846–1914) was an inventor and business giant. He invented the first air brake, which made rail travel safer. His company produced lightbulbs, appliances, generators, and steam engines, among other products. He lived in Wilmerding.

August Wilson (1945–2005) was a playwright who set his works in his hometown of Pittsburgh. He won the Pulitzer Prize for Drama twice, for *Fences* and *The Piano Lesson*.

Will Smith

RESOURCES

BOOKS

Nonfiction

Burgan, Michael. *Valley Forge*. Minneapolis: Compass Point Books, 2004.

Cousins, Margaret. *Ben Franklin of Old Philadelphia*. New York: Random House, 2004.

Elish, Dan. *The Battle of Gettysburg*. Danbury, Conn.: Children's Press, 2005.

Gray, Edward G. *Colonial America: A History in Documents*. New York: Oxford University Press, 2002.

Hinman, Bonnie. *Pennsylvania: William Penn and the City of Brotherly Love*. Hockessin, Del.: Mitchell Lane Publishers, 2006.

Murphy, Jim. *An American Plague: The True and Terrifying Story of the Yellow Fever Epidemic of 1793*. New York: Clarion Books, 2003.

Nobleman, Marc Tyler. *The Johnstown Flood*. Minneapolis: Compass Point Books, 2005.

Wiener, Roberta. *Pennsylvania: The History of Pennsylvania Colony, 1681–1776*. Chicago: Raintree, 2004.

Fiction

Curtis, Alice Turner. *Yankee Girl at Gettysburg*. Bedford, Mass.: Applewood Books, 1999.

De Angeli, Marguerite. *Thee, Hannah!* Scottdale, Pa.: Herald Press, 2000.

Fritz, Jean. *The Cabin Faced West*. New York: Putnam Juvenile, 2001.

Gregory, Kristiana. *The Winter of Red Snow: The Revolutionary War Diary of Abigail Jane Stewart, Valley Forge, Pennsylvania, 1777*. New York: Scholastic, 1996.

Gross, Virginia T. *The Day It Rained Forever: A Story of the Johnstown Flood*. New York: Puffin, 1993.

Lawson, Robert. *Ben and Me: An Astonishing Life of Benjamin Franklin by His Good Mouse Amos*. New York: Little, Brown Young Readers, 1988.

DVDs

Civil War Battlefields. Timeless Media Group, 2007.
Discoveries … America: Pennsylvania. Bennett-Watt Entertainment, 2003.
Historic Travel U.S.—Pennsylvania Marches On. Tapeworm Video, 2005.

WEB SITES AND ORGANIZATIONS

The Battle of Gettysburg

www.civilwarhome.com/gettysbu.htm
Step back in history and read Gettysburg battle overviews, the Order of Battle for both the Union and Confederate armies at Gettysburg, and more.

Commonwealth of Pennsylvania

www.state.pa.us
Visit this official site that provides state-related news and information for citizens, visitors, and businesses.

Delaware (Lenni Lenape) Tribe of Indians

www.delawaretribeofindians.nsn.us
Visit the official Web site of the Lenape people. This site includes information about the dances, history, clothing, and humor of the Lenni Lenape people.

Enchanted Learning: Pennsylvania—Facts, Map and State Symbols

www.enchantedlearning.com/usa/states/pennsylvania
Collect more facts about Pennsylvania.

Historic Valley Forge

www.ushistory.org/valleyforge
Learn more about Valley Forge from the Valley Forge Historical Society.

Independence Hall

www.ushistory.org/tour/tour_indhall.htm
Visit the site where the Declaration of Independence was signed and adopted.

The Life of William Penn

www.2020site.org/penn/index.html
Read about William Penn, a tireless writer who expounded his theories on religious tolerance and the Quaker ideals in books, essays, and pamphlets.

PBS: Benjamin Franklin

www.pbs.org/benfranklin
Learn all about the printer, inventor, patriot, and diplomat.

The Pennsylvania General Assembly

www.legis.state.pa.us
Learn about Pennsylvania's capitol and the General Assembly.

INDEX

★ ★ ★

AUTHOR'S TIPS AND SOURCE NOTES

★ ★ ★

Research for *Pennsylvania* began with *William Penn and the Founding of Pennsylvania, 1680–1684: A Documentary History*, edited by Jean R. Soderlund. Pennsylvania had an unusual beginning, and the documents in this source were particularly interesting. *Benjamin Franklin, Pennsylvania, and the First Nations: The Treaties of 1736–62*, edited by Susan Kalter, helped in understanding the relationship between the state's Native people and colonists.

For general information, try *Our Pennsylvania* by Jerry Irwin or *Pennsylvania: A History of the Commonwealth*, edited by Randall M. Miller and William A. Pencak. Both sources provide extensive detail about the state's history and are available through your local library. To get a feel for the state's cities, towns, and attractions, look at Pennsylvania travel guides by Moon and Fodor and *Pennsylvania Firsts: The Famous, Infamous, and Quirky of the Keystone State* by Patrick M. Reynolds.

I used many Internet sites in my research. The best ones were the Commonwealth of Pennsylvania (www.state.pa.us) and the Pennsylvania General Assembly (www.legis.state.pa.us), which also has information on the state's history. In addition, I used Explore Pennsylvania History (www.explorepahistory.com) and the site at www.ushistory.org/Pennsylvania. For primary sources, the Historical Society of Pennsylvania (www.hsp.org/default.aspx?id = 394) is a good place to start.